Castles in England and Wales

Castles in England and Wales

W. Douglas Simpson

B. T. Batsford Limited

First published 1969
7134 0613 5

Printed in Great Britain by
The Aberdeen University Press, Aberdeen
and bound by Kemp Hall Bindery Ltd, Oxford
for the publishers
B.T. Batsford Limited
4 Fitzhardinge Street London W 1

Contents

	Acknowledgment	vii
	Note	ix
1	The Meaning of Castles in English History	1
2	A Pageant of English Castellar Construction	15
3	Norman Castles of Timbered Earthwork	28
4	Stone Keeps of Norman and Angevin Times	52
5	Norman Town and Castle Planning	80
6	Castles of Enceinte	87
7	Master James of St George and the Edwardian Castles	104
8	The Northern Tower Houses	126
9	Castles in Brick	136
10	Bastard Feudalism and the Latest Castles	150
11	The Fighting Finish of the English Castle	163
	Index	170

Acknowledgment

The author and publishers thank the following for their kind permission to reproduce the photographs included in this book. Aerofilms Limited for figures 3, 4, 19, 21, 24, 28 and 35; the late Brian C. Clayton for figures 6, 11, 13, 15, 16, 23, 30, 33 and 36; J. Dixon-Scott for figure 31; Leonard and Marjorie Gayton for figure 17; Humphrey and Vera Joel for figure 18; A. F. Kersting for figures 1, 5, 7, 8, 9, 12, 14, 20, 22, 25, 26, 29 and 32; Nottingham Public Libraries for figure 2; Royal Commission on Historical Monuments (England) Crown Copyright for figure 27; the late Will F. Taylor for figure 10.

All the plans have been drawn by Peter Fraser and we acknowledge with thanks the sources on which these plans are based: Royal Commission on Ancient Monuments (Anglesey) H.M. Stationery Office for Beaumaris Castle ground plan; Royal Commission on Ancient Monuments (Essex), H.M. Stationery Office for the plan of the section through the keep and floor plans of Hedingham Castle; Royal Commission on Ancient Monuments (Flintshire), H.M. Stationery Office for Rhuddlan Castle ground plan; Ministry of Works pamphlets, H.M. Stationery Office for the plans of Caernarvon Castle and Colchester Castle, (all by permission of the Controller of H.M. Stationery Office) *English Medieval Castles* by R. Allen Brown published by B. T. Batsford Limited for the plans of Caerphilly and Conisbrough Castles (after G. T. Clark), and Oxford Castle based on drawings by H. Munro Cautley; *Journal of the British Archaeological Association* for the plan of Buckden Palace; *Lewes Castle* by Walter H. Godfrey published by the Sussex Archaeological Society; Victoria County History for the plan of Bolton Castle; Transactions of the Thoroton Society of Nottinghamshire Volume XLVII 1943 for the plan of Wollaton Hall.

Note

Since the last war there has been a marked upsurge of interest in our ancient castles. It has been shown in the amount of attention devoted to them in our illustrated magazines, in radio and television programmes, even in our postage stamps. Above all it has been shown in a spate of books.

Most of these have been concerned primarily with the architectural development of the medieval castle. The responsibility for adding yet another to the number of books upon this subject must lie with my publishers. Its justification may be found in the fact that the present work aims not only at giving a fair picture of the origin, development and decline of the English castle, but also to set forth the part that our castles have played in the political and social evolution of England and Wales; and to give some account, albeit in summary fashion, of the history of each castle selected for treatment. Inevitably, the process of selection has been a severe one. Many famous and imposing castles will find no place, other than perhaps bare mention, in the following chapters. In making my choice I have been guided throughout by the theme and pattern of the book as above set forth.

W.D.S.

I

The Meaning of Castles in English History

Our literary critics seem in general agreed that *Ivanhoe* cannot be numbered among the greatest of the Waverley Novels: for the reason that, in writing it, Sir Walter Scott was not drawing, as in the Scottish romances, from his own personal knowledge and experience of the life and characteristics of his fellow countrymen, but was basing his narrative on book learning. And for this reason, *Ivanhoe* has proved itself far more vulnerable to the assaults of the stickler for antiquarian accuracy than the novels that deal with Scottish history and manners during the sixteenth, seventeenth and eighteenth centuries—times, after all, which lay fairly close to the novelist's own age, and concerning which he could draw upon his vast stores of intimate knowledge garnered from his own reading and observation, and from traditions yet to be had for the gleaning. So Freeman has pointed out how the root-conception of *Ivanhoe*, that of a great gulf fixed between Norman conqueror and Saxon conquered, still persisting in Richard the Lion-Heart's reign, is mistaken, and that Cedric the Saxon and Athelstane of Coningsburgh are impossible figures for their time. Other critics have followed Freeman in compiling an imposing list of secondary anachronisms. The famous tournament at Ashby-de-la-Zouch, they urge, is depicted with a splendour more in keeping with the fourteenth century than with the twelfth; Scott's heraldry is also of the latter period; the longbow, which performs such astounding feats in the hands of Locksley and his rival Hubert, was not introduced into England until the reign of the first Edward; there are similar blunders in the description of dress and armour; the great Tower of Coningsburgh is not a Saxon castle of the Heptarchy, but was newly built by Norman masons about the very time of the story; and so on and so forth.

Amid all this clamour of pedantic fault-finding we are apt to lose sight of the fact that many of these inaccuracies were perfectly well known to Scott himself. In his Dedicatory Epistle he candidly admits that he may have 'confused the manners of two or three centuries'. What he set out to do was to provide his readers with a generalised picture of the Middle Ages—viewed, of course, through the rose-tinted glasses of the Romantic Revival. He was the first to essay such a task. How successful was his achievement is evident if we but stop to consider the enormous influence exerted by *Ivanhoe* not merely upon Sir Walter's own generation, but upon subsequent times. So consummate is the Wizard's artistry that even today, as I read this brave old yarn for the *n*th time, all the historical and antiquarian solecisms fall out of recollection, and the illusion of reality is complete until the last page is turned and the book once again put back on its shelf. *Ivanhoe* may indeed be the product of book learning, I think as my critical faculty re-asserts itself; but it certainly does not smell of the lamp. And for the great public at large, who are neither versed in history nor apt in medieval studies, it is not too much to say that the popular conception of the Middle Ages, with their castles and monasteries, their barons, churchmen, yeomen and serfs, their joustings and feastings, their tinsel and their drab, can be traced back almost to a single well-spring: *Ivanhoe*. Even that most modern and sophisticated of the arts, the cinema, when it comes to deal with a medieval theme, appears to look back to *Ivanhoe* for its stage setting and its properties. And the main characters in the story—Front-de-Boeuf and Bois-Guilbert, Gurth, Wamba, Locksley, Prior Aymer, the Holy Clerk of Copmanhurst, Isaac of York and all the rest—each and all of them have a numerous and thriving progeny, surviving into the fiction writing of our own time. They are all types—types of the Middle Ages as the man in the street imagines them. Only in one instance has Scott risen above this parade of medieval pageantry, and in the Jewess Rebecca depicted for us a woman who, it seems to me, deserves a modest rank among the select and timeless company of tragic heroines which is headed by Antigone and Tess of the D'Urbervilles.

And yet, despite all that a rigid antiquarianism can urge against

Ivanhoe, one finds, not once but often in its pages, how Scott's un-rivalled intuition has seized and brought out some cardinal point, some vital truth, in medieval life. For example, there is a deep verity in the contrast he draws between the moated homestead of the Saxon Cedric, with its timbered hall, and the ponderous stone tower of Front-de-Boeuf's Norman castle. Rotherwood, we are told, is 'a low irregular building, containing several courtyards or enclosures, extending over a considerable space of ground, and which, though its size argued the inhabitant to be a person of wealth, differed entirely from

Timbered earthworks from the Bayeux Tapestry

the tall turreted and castellated buildings in which the Norman nobility resided, and which had become the universal style of architecture throughout England'. The main feature of Cedric's mansion, as it is further described to us, is the hall, with its dais on which the high table was set, off which opened the private apartments of the owner, while at the lower end of the hall were doors communicating with the exterior and with the kitchen and service accommodation. By contrast, the main feature of Torquilstone Castle is 'a donjon, or large and high square tower, surrounded by buildings of inferior height, which were encircled by an inner courtyard'. True, the contrasting picture which Sir Walter here draws is somewhat less than the truth; for it is now recognised that the tall stone donjon was not the sole, nay it was not even the usual type of Norman castle in vogue during Coeur-de-Lion's time. Most of these castles were made not of stone and lime but of earth and timber. They consisted of a wooden tower set within a log palisade upon a scarped mound surrounded by a ditch. This is the type of castle which the Normans called a *motte*. It alone is depicted on the Bayeux Tapestry; and in this woven record again we have the contrast between the tall Norman castles on their *mottes* and the low horizontal *aula* or hall of the Saxon Harold. Attached to the moated mound, or sometimes wholly enclosing it, was a bailey and courtyard, likewise ditched, banked, and palisaded. This served to shelter the subsidiary buildings of the manorial establishment. Throughout Norman times such timbered earthworks were the prevailing type of castle; while the heavy stone tower was exceptional, and did not become common until the twelfth century was far spent. Nevertheless, the contrast between *aula* and *turris*, between Rotherwood and Torquilstone, is true and fundamental. An understanding of this is vital to the study of the medieval castle—and indeed, as will be noted in Chapter 8, to a comprehension of the evolution of the English country-house from Norman times to the present day.

By definition, the castle is the private stronghold of a feudal lord. In its fully developed form, the feudal system was introduced into this country by the Norman conquerors. Wherever a Norman baron settled down, there he threw up a castle as a fortified residence in which he could maintain himself against his rivals and against the Saxon peasantry. Beside the castle he would build a chapel for the convenience of his family and household and the tenants who huddled for protection under the skirts of the castle ramparts. As often as not, the priest serving this chapel would be a younger brother or other kinsman of the lord of the manor. In due course the manor might thus come to be a parish; the castle chapel would grow into the parish church; and church and castle, side by side, would stand for the ecclesiastical and temporal *fulcra* of the early parochial organisation. To the present day that ancient association of manor and parish, castle and church, so important for the early development of our local institutions, is seen on the face of England in the frequency with which the remains of a Norman castle are found hard by an ancient parish church.

In the nature of the case, feudalism was a product of weak government. The Germanic monarchies which arose on the soil of the old Roman Empire were not able to discharge the military, administrative, financial and judicial responsibilities of government in the efficient and centralised manner of the imperial administration. Nor could they maintain the *pax Romana*—which indeed had become a thing of the past long before the fall of the Western Empire. So they had to compromise by delegating to the great local magnates many of the functions proper to a central government. Long centuries would pass ere the modern state, resuming the responsibilities that the decaying Roman Empire had abdicated, could impose law and order upon its lieges on its own account, instead of through the feudal magnates. When that day came the feudal castle had outlived its purpose. Its work was done and it sank into ruins, or was transformed into a stately country house. From circumstances familiar to all students of our history, a relatively strong central government emerged upon English soil at an earlier date than elsewhere in Europe. In consequence of this, the feudal castle, in its strictly military sense, was already becoming an anachronism by the middle of the fourteenth century. Great houses built castle-wise continued indeed to be erected, but largely as a matter of prestige. By the end of the fifteenth century, the strong Tudor monarchs had put paid to the castle as the military stronghold of a wealthy landowner. Probably the last English castle to be erected with a serious defensible intent was Thornbury in Gloucestershire, left unfinished by Edward Stafford, Duke of Buckingham, on his execution in 1521, as an 'over mighty subject', by Henry VIII.

Yet, in spite of the silent warning conveyed by the half-built towers of Thornbury, and despite the Tudor mansion-houses that adorned the land in the spacious days of Elizabeth I, the idea of castellar construction as the proper portrayal of a great landlord's pride found a last and astonishing manifestation in Wollaton Hall, near Nottingham, the magnificent mansion erected by Sir Francis Willoughby between 1580 and 1588, at the then enormous cost of £80,000. Although he came of an ancient, though far from famous line, he had himself little claim to distinction other than his enormous wealth, derived from his interest in the Nottingham iron and coal mines. A ground plan and part elevation appear among John Thorpe's drawings, and there is every reason to acclaim that great Elizabethan architect as the designer of Wollaton Hall. Even at this late date the scheme of the house betrays a curious, and evidently deliberate, harking back to medieval ideas. It consists, as it were, of a central square 'keep', surrounded by four *corps de logis* with square angle towers. But there is no internal court-yard. The whole building is solid; and the 'keep', lofty and massive, is

Plan of Wollaton Hall

raised above a large central hall, round which the living apartments are grouped. This hall is carried up to a height of 53 feet, and its windows are kept high (35 feet above the floor!) with plunged soles, like the windows of a clearstorey, in order to overlook the two-storeyed rooms by which the hall is enclosed. In fact, the hall is well on the way to becoming nothing more than a magnificent vestibule; and although in Thorpe's design it was still intended for banqueting or as a ball-room, and was entered at the lower end through a screen under a music gallery in the traditional way, yet the vestibular conception, so strongly suggested by the lay-out, received full acknowledgment in Sir Jeffry Wyatville's alterations, whereby the hall has been provided with doors set midway in each side. From the hall, in the original scheme, doors admitted to the apartments all round, and also to a stately stair by which the upper storeys of the mansion were reached. The hammer-beam construction of the hall roof is another medieval survival, though it is here tricked out in the garb of the Renaissance. Medievalism also is subtly apparent in the external features of the house: for whereas the *corps de logis* or lower portions and the angle towers are carried out in the aggressive, over-decorated quasiclassical style in vogue at the time, the upper portions of the 'keep' are pierced with large bastard Gothic windows, and at its four corners are corbelled angle turrets quite in the Gothic fashion. Medievalism also lurks, even more surprisingly in Elizabethan England, in a well-preserved prison in the basement; while the rock-hewn subterranean cellarage reminds one perfectly of the gloomy vaulted fastnesses of a feudal castle.

Mr J. A. Gotch remarks of Wollaton Hall that 'its plan places it in a category almost by itself'. Mr Avray Tipping labours to explain it as an elaboration of 'the complete and typical H-shaped Elizabethan house plan'. To Mr Nathaniel Lloyd it is just 'a freak house'. In so far as it is built castle-wise, Wollaton Hall is less a freak than a whimsy. As to its plan, all the puzzlement is simply due to the fact, as I have pointed out elsewhere, that it has not been recognised for what it is—an example, perhaps unique in England, of the French plan *tout une masse*, as expounded by Jacques Androuet du Cerceau in his famous book, *Les Plus Excellens Bastiments de France*, published in two volumes in 1576 and 1579. Unquestionably Thorpe got the idea for Wollaton from du Cerceau's book, of which his album betrays close study.[1]

The enthusiasm for the Middle Ages generated by the publication of *Ivanhoe* had some curious results. Of these perhaps the most remarkable was the tournament held at Eglinton Castle, Ayrshire, in 1839—a bizarre affair modelled upon the Gentle and Joyous Passage of Arms of Ashby-de-la-Zouch. One of the mail-clad knights who on that day

[1] *Proc. Soc. Ant. Scot.*, vol. LXXXVI, pp. 70–80.

clashed in the lists was the future Emperor Napoleon III; while the part of *La Rayne de la Beaulte et des Amours* was played by Lady Seymour, a grand-daughter of Sheridan. A more enduring result of the *Ivanhoe* craze was the building of one or two major country seats as replicas of a medieval castle. Of these we may here mention only two. Near Bangor in Caernarvonshire, Penrhyn Castle was built in 1827–47 after the pattern of a Norman castle, with a huge five-storeyed keep. This remarkable reproduction is said to have cost Lord Penrhyn no less than half a million pounds! And in Cheshire, on the summit of an abrupt wooded hill, Anthony Salvin built, in the mid-nineteenth century, Peckforton Castle to the order of the first Lord Tollemache. This astonishing structure is a complete replica of a thirteenth-century castle. The curtain walls and towers rise from the slopes, so that the courtyard, on the flattened summit, is at a considerably higher level, with a great hall, chapel and domestic apartments grouped picturesquely round it.

More legitimate, perhaps, than such *tours de force* is the scholarly restoration of a medieval castle to fit it once more for use as a habitable dwelling. Nowhere in Britain has this been done on the lavish scale of Pierrefonds or Hautkoenigsbourg. Perhaps the most striking example is Castell Coch in Glamorgan, one of the most remarkable of Welsh castles. It dates from the thirteenth century, and consists of a triangular courtyard with two rounded sides, defended by three strong cylindrical towers. The castle was restored in the last century by the Marquess of Bute. It is said to contain a secret treasure guarded by three enormous ravens. Another large-scale modern restoration is that of Herstmonceux Castle, Sussex, to be discussed in Chapter 9. Mention may also be made of Allington Castle, built under royal licence in 1281, and beautifully restored in the present century by Sir William Martin-Conway. But more space must be provided for considering the most remarkable modern restoration of an English baronial fortalice, Hever Castle in Kent.

Since the reign of Henry II it had been the law of England that no baron could erect a castle without obtaining a licence from the king. It is easy to understand that this salutary enactment was often more honoured in the breach than in the observance; particularly in times when the Crown was weak, as in the anarchy under Stephen. Such documents were styled 'licences to crenellate'—crenellation being the battlements crowning a tower or a curtain wall. A licence to crenellate his house at Hever was granted to Sir Stephen de Penchester in 1272. Much of the 'fore-face' of the castle seems to have been erected subsequently to that date. About 1340 a second licence was granted to William de Hever, and to this period may be ascribed the imposing machicolated war-head of the gate-house. Subsequently the manor was held by Sir John Fastolf and Sir Roger Fiennes, two magnates to whom respectively we owe the building of the famous brick castles of Caister and Herstmonceux, to be considered in Chapter 9. In 1462 Hever passed by purchase to the Boleyn family. It was at Hever Castle that Henry VIII courted his second wife, Anne Boleyn. Never before of great importance, the Boleyns of Hever sank back into obscurity after Queen Anne's bloody death: and their principal claim to distinction is that through her they became the ancestors of her daughter, Elizabeth I, and so of our present Royal Family. On the death of Anne's father in 1539 King Henry granted Hever to his fourth wife, Anne of Cleves, whom he had just divorced. Its subsequent history need not detain us until 1903, when the castle, by this time much decayed, was bought by Mr William Waldorf Astor, later created Viscount Astor of Hever. The new owner restored the castle, flooded the moat, diverted the River Eden so as to create an artificial lake of 35 acres, and over against the castle, which is quite small, built a delightful 'village' in Tudor style to house his guests and dependents. The result must be considered as one of the most imaginative and successful restorations of a medieval castle that England can boast.

Set within its watery cincture, and backed by the picturesque array of half-timbered gables, tiled roofs and quaintly varied chimneys of the 'Tudor village', Hever Castle, though small in size, offers an imposing front to the visitor who approaches it across the timber bridge that spans the moat. Built of good coursed pink local rubble, the fore-face of the castle presents an imposing central machicolated gatehouse with an embattled parapet, while on either hand it is terminated by tall slender towers, likewise crenellated but without machicolations. The gatehouse belongs to a type which we shall have to consider when we come to deal with the Edwardian castles: that is to say, it combines the functions of a well-defended 'house of entry' with the principal dwelling rooms of the lord of the manor. Besides a drawbridge, there were no less than three portcullises, and two strong iron-studded doorways.

Most of the buildings which surround the courtyard had been re-fashioned by the Boleyns. The north range, over against the entrance, contains the great hall, with the kitchen at its eastern end; while from the opposite or dais end opened the lord's private apartments in the western range, superseding the fourteenth-century suite in the gate-house. All these apartments were extensively, yet most sympathetically restored by Viscount Astor. Enriched internally and in its purlieus by many artistic treasures, and enclosed in spacious landscaped grounds, Hever Castle today combines the romantic glamour of the Middle Ages with the cultured grace of the Renaissance and all the convenience and comfort of a well-appointed modern mansion-house. Alas! the rapidly changing circumstances of our twentieth century have rendered it certain that such an aesthetic *tour de force* is unlikely to be repeated in England.

The colonnaded Italian garden with its rock-cut grottoes, its walls of mellow honey-coloured stone, its antique and Renaissance marbles, whose virginal white contrasts with the warm tone of the masonry; the green of the shorn hedges and clustering foliage; the flashing fountains and the pond gay with water-lilies—all combine to form a scene of cultured and restful beauty. On a fine hot summer's day how complete is the illusion of Italy in Kent! Yet to remind us where we are, over the trees to the south-west rises the graceful, typically English spire of St Peter's parish church, which contains perhaps the most beautiful of all our brasses, commemorating Margaret Cheyne, who died in 1419; and also the magnificent brass of Sir Thomas Boleyn, the father of Queen Anne, portraying him with the robes and insignia of the Order of the Garter.

From what has been said in these introductory pages, my readers will already have understood that our castles, whether ruined or otherwise, are something more than merely a conspicuous and picturesque element in the English countryside, or even than the scene of events famous in English history. They are also deeply embedded in the origins of our English institutions.

Sentiment apart, the relations between a modern landlord and his tenants are primarily economic. The tenant pays the rent and the land-lord receives it. Both landlord and tenant are bound by statutory

obligations to each other; and in this particular aspect of their relations the modern omnicompetent state tends to interfere more and more, not always to the advantage of either. By contrast, the feudal landlord, in addition to exacting rents (mostly in kind) from his tenants, was charged with the powers of local government over them. In his barony courts he judged them, alike in criminal and in civil cases; and in time of war his tenantry assembled in the castle court and marched forth under their lord's banner to join the national army. Feudalism was thus a system whereby ownership of land was burdened with the responsibility for local government and national defence.

It is easy to understand that such a system placed great power in the hands of the magnates, and could lead to sore oppression of their vassals. Ill treatment of this sort was of course rifest under a weak monarch. Everyone is familiar with the terrible results of the anarchy under Stephen, when men cried out in their despair that Christ and His Saints were asleep. The oft-quoted passage from the Anglo-Saxon Chronicle has found a place in many books upon English castles. The annalist tells us, in horrifying terms, how every powerful man built himself a castle, and how the castles were filled with devils and evil men:

> They hanged up men by the feet, and smoked them with foul smoke; some were hanged up by their thumbs, others by their head, and coats of mail were hung on to their feet. They put knotted strings about men's heads, and twisted them till they went to the brain. They put men into prisons where adders and toads were crawling, and so they tormented them. Some they put into a chest, short and narrow and not deep, and that had sharp stones within; and forced men therein, so that they broke all their limbs. In many of the castles were hateful and grim things called neckties, which two or three men had enough to do to carry. This instrument of torture was thus made: it was fastened to a beam, and a sharp iron to go about a man's neck and throat, so that he might no way sit or lie or sleep, but he bore all the iron. Many thousands they starved with hunger.

It is indeed a fearsome picture, and ever since it has darkened the popular impression of our castles—even in our own day, which has witnessed deeds of cruelty on a scale and to a degree that would have horrified the men of the Middle Ages. Yet it is never fair to judge an institution by its perversion or abuse. A calmer judgment will discover

3 Hever Castle

an ethical justification for the feudal system, and will recognise in it the
seed-bed of many of our most valued institutions.

The land improvers of the nineteenth century, and the business
magnates of the Industrial Revolution, had few statutory obligations for
the welfare of those by whose toil their wealth was won. Hence the
dark Satanic mills and the sad slums of our cities; hence the dispossession
of rural communities to make way for improved agricultural methods
more economical in man-power. Both processes resulted in great social
hardships, to correct which the modern state has intervened. By contrast,
the medieval landlord could not evade his feudal responsibility for his
tenants. Both shared a common interest. The stronger the power of the
feudal magnate, the firmer his protection and government of his
tenantry, the more his tenantry would prosper; the greater their prosperity, the greater grew his wealth, and therefore his power to protect
them and to advance their welfare. And for every 'bad baron' of the
Front-de-Boeuf type, it was easy to compile, from manor-court
records and other contemporary sources, many instances of feudal.
magnates who, according to the standards of their time, looked after
their vassals with paternal benevolence. Our Universities, our public
schools and grammar schools, our almshouses and charitable foundations, our churches great and small, owe more to the encastled magnates
of feudal England than is often recognised.

Again, the feudal system was a prime nursery of self-government
The baron's court provided a training ground in local administration,
finance and law, which in due course became available to the royal
sheriff or itinerant judge. Upon a national scale, out of the royal Great
Council of feudal tenants-in-chief grew, in course of time, the British
Parliament. In the intermediate stage, the major feudal magnates maintained 'households', as they were called, namely organisations in which
all the functions of the King's government, alike civil, judicial and
military, were reproduced on a smaller scale. Thus an ever-increasing
number of officials were being trained in the work of local and regional
government; with the result that when under the Tudors the central
government finally prevailed over the ruins of a feudalism destroyed in
the Wars of the Roses, the new 'Grand Monarchy', which guided the
process of transforming England from a medieval to a modern state,
found to its hand a wealth of trained administrative talent probably not
excelled, at that time, elsewhere in Europe. We must therefore

recognise in our castles the administrative centres of a system out of which the modern governance of England has largely grown.

Of all the feudal magnates of course the foremost was the King. Therefore in principle the royal castles were in no way distinct from the castles of the barons. Each was the centre of the same sort of military, fiscal, administrative and judicial arrangements. Yet in the nature of things the royal castles came to resemble state fortresses of the modern type, built, maintained and garrisoned to subserve national ends. This is especially the case in the great castles erected by Edward I to secure his conquests in Wales. Others again emerged as national fortresses by virtue of their strategic position, such as Dover, which Hubert de Burgh described as 'the key of England'. Others again, like Corfe Castle or the Tower of London, have earned for themselves a sombre fame as state prisons.

Finally, a word of caution. The medieval castle is obviously a strong fortalice; yet it is a mistake to exaggerate its military aspect. It is a great error to think of a castle in the Middle Ages as constantly manned in instant readiness for war. No castle was ever maintained by a garrison after the fashion imagined by Sir Walter Scott:

> They quitted not their harness bright,
> Neither by day nor yet by night:
> They lay down to rest,
> With corslet laced,
> Pillowed on buckler cold and hard;
> They carved at the meal
> With gloves of steel,
> And they drank the red wine through the helmet barred.

In sober fact, the medieval castle was first and foremost a country gentleman's seat, upon which the needs of a scambling and unquiet time imposed a fortified carapace. It was not normally armed to the teeth or stuffed with a garrison of professional soldiers, each at his action station. In time of peace it would contain simply the lord's *familia* or household. During his frequent absences, no more than a caretaker and a few servants would be at hand. In time of war the castle would be garrisoned by the lord's tenantry who dwelt around, and could be called up under the feudal obligation known as 'castle guard'. Sometimes, as in the case of a royal castle, different towers were assigned to specified vassals, who in respect of the tenure of their lands were bound to garrison each his allotted tower in time of war. Thus some of the towers at Dover Castle are still called by the names of the crown vassals who had to furnish their garrisons.

In the following pages we shall aim to consider our castles not merely as specimens of 'military architecture', nor as the scenes of events famous in history, but also as centres of feudal government, as the outward and visible signs of a system that has left a deep imprint on English history—a system the traces of which, despite all the cumulative changes of modern time, still bulk large in our present institutions.

2
A Pageant of English Castellar Construction

In this chapter I propose to consider three major castles—two of them famous throughout the British Isles and far beyond; the third, most undeservedly, much less well known. Kenilworth and Warwick are the two grandest castles of the Midlands, and their names are deeply etched into the panorama of English history. Caldicot in Monmouthshire, on the marshy northern shore of the Severn estuary, can boast much less of historical renown, but was held by a long succession of famous and not seldom tragic lords. Considered together, these three notable buildings afford us a complete conspectus of the development of the English castle from Norman *motte* to Tudor palace; so that a study of the group provides us, as it were, with a vignette of our whole theme.

Let us begin with CALDICOT. In the Domesday survey, this manor, of considerable extent, was held by Durand, Sheriff of Gloucester. By him, no doubt, was thrown up the moated mound that occupies the north-west corner of the castle. Subsequently Caldicot passed to the great Norman family of de Bohun, Earls of Hereford, by whom it was held until 1377. The most famous of these puissant magnates was Humphrey de Bohun, third Earl of Hereford, who held the hereditary post of Constable of England. With his colleague in high office of state, the Earl Marshal, he led the baronial opposition to Edward I. Their defiant refusal to join in the King's Flemish campaign of 1297 is a dramatic incident in English history. The King broke out into one of those demonic rages to which the Plantagenets were prone. 'By God, Sir Earl', he shouted at his Marshal, 'you shall either go or hang' 'By God, Sir King', stormed back the Earl of Norfolk, 'I will neither go nor hang!' Both Constable and Marshal resigned their offices, and mobilised their feudal levies; so that Edward had to sail for Flanders without them. In the upshot, the revolt of Wallace in Scotland drove the overbearing King to come to terms with the baronial opposition. The Confirmation of the Charters, which followed before the year was out, is rightly hailed as 'one of the great turning points in the history of our constitution'.

In the course of the Bohun ownership the early Norman mount and bailey was extended, and converted into a formidable castle of stone. First to be built was the circular donjon, of beautiful masonry, by which the *motte* is crowned, It exhibits the peculiarity, paralleled in the same county at Skenfrith Castle, of possessing a semicircular excrescence on the side exterior to the bailey, apparently solid in the main, but possessing a prison in the basement. The donjon itself comprises three storeys of well-appointed living rooms, above a ground floor doubtless used for storage. The door is on the first floor, and from it, on the one side, a mural stair, circling round in the circumference of the wall (in the early fashion as at Conisbrough, see p. 72) descends to the store; while on the other side of the entrance a spiral stair mounts to the two upper floors, above which a third stair, again following the curvature of the wall, leads up to the battlements. Altogether this is a most finished tower. Clearly it was designed to be the lord's residence. The architectural detail indicates a date about the close of the twelfth century.

To this tower, in the course of the next century, massive curtain walls were added so as to enclose an extended bailey, with a powerful horse-shoe shaped tower at the south-east angle, a smaller round tower at the south-west angle, and a postern tower, likewise round, midway on the west front. Upon the horse-shoe tower the battlements are well preserved, also the corbels and putlog holes for a timber war-head. In the postern tower the entrance opens on the flank, so as to give a right-angled turn, thus checking a direct inrush. Early in the fourteenth century a splendid gatehouse was added on the south front. Built of fine ashlar, this forms an oblong structure with square latrine towers on either flank. The entrance passage is well defended by an external pit, two pairs of portcullises, and two pairs of folding doors; but it is noteworthy that the inner pair of folding doors do not close against the courtyard, nor in the upper floors is there a fine hall such as forms a feature of the Edwardian keep-gatehouses, which we shall discuss in Chapter 7. Nevertheless, the upper storeys of this noble gatehouse contain a suite of handsome living rooms. Clearly it was meant to supersede the old donjon as the quarters of the lord or castellan. The architectural details of the gatehouse are very ornate. The parapet corbels are finely carved as human heads. Two of them are crowned, and have been thought to be portraits of the unlucky Edward II and his Queen, the 'she-wolf of France'.

About the same time a postern tower, three-sided towards the field, was added on the opposite side of the courtyard. Later in the fourteenth century a handsome hall was erected on the east of the gatehouse, the curtain being rebuilt so as to admit a noble row of traceried windows. All this fine work must be assigned to the Bohun ownership, which terminated in 1377, when, the male line having failed, Caldicot passed to Thomas of Woodstock, Duke of Gloucester, the youngest son of Edward III. The Prince had married the Bohun heiress, and stood high in his ageing father's favour: but the story of his quarrel with Richard II, and his murder under trust by his royal nephew's order in 1398, forms one of the painful episodes in that monarch's unhappy reign. Readers of Shakespeare's *Richard II* will remember how Gloucester's widow makes eloquent plaint to the murdered Duke's brother, John of Gaunt:

> Edward's seven sons, whereof thyself art one,
> Were as seven vials of his sacred blood,
> Or seven fair branches springing from one root;
> Some of these seven are dried by nature's course,
> Some of these branches by the Destinies cut:
> But Thomas, my dear lord, my life, my Gloucester,
> One vial full of Edward's sacred blood,
> One flourishing branch of his most royal root,
> Is cracked, and all the precious liquor spilt,
> Is hacked down, and his summer leaves all faded,
> By envy's hand, and murder's bloody axe.

Subsequently Caldicot passed to the ducal house of Buckingham—a line which in its turn ended in tragedy, when in 1521 Edward Stafford, third Duke of Buckingham, fell a victim to the jealousy of Henry

VIII.[1] By 1613 Caldicot Castle was in utter decay, and had been so, time out of mind. What seems like a deliberate breach in the east curtain is therefore less likely to have been made in the Civil War than during the Wars of the Roses, in the course of which the first Duke of Buckingham fell in battle and the second was beheaded by Richard III. In modern times the gatehouse has been fitted up as a noble residence. Thus reconstituted, the long south front of Caldicot Castle, flanked by its two stout circular towers and dominated centrally by the brow-beating gatehouse, is surely one of the finest examples of English castle work. And the charm of the wide-spreading pile is enhanced by the varied tint and texture of its masonry.

As seen from a little distance, and from almost every viewpoint, KENILWORTH CASTLE is frankly a vast, red, ugly ruin. This arises chiefly from the amorphous lumpy effect of the main masses and their bald horizontal wall-heads, which give the ruins something of the aspect of a burnt-out factory, with nothing of the picturesqueness of ruined gable battlement and turret that usually marks an ancient castle. It is only when one approaches nearer, and examines the buildings in detail, that one realises, not only their extreme stylistic beauty, but also the fact that the work of each period—Norman keep, mural towers of the thirteenth century, John of Gaunt's palace, and the various buildings added by Dudley—are, each and all, the creations of great masters of design and execution. In almost no other English castle has there been, through the whole sequence from Norman to Tudor times, such sustained excellence alike in conception and in execution.

The founder of the castle was Geoffrey de Clinton, Treasurer to Henry I. At first it was a timbered earthwork of the type which we have already encountered at Caldicot, and must now consider more carefully *apropos* of Kenilworth and Warwick. The replacement of the palisades by stone walls and towers was mainly the work of King John. Later in the thirteenth century the demesne of Kenilworth was held by no less a person than the great Earl of Leicester, Simon de Montfort. After his death on the battlefield of Evesham (1265) some of his adherents held the castle against Henry III in one of the greatest sieges in

---

[1] See *supra*, p. 5.

English history. Every resource of assault, battery and ballistics was employed by both attackers and defenders—including a naval assault across the lake by barges brought over from Chester. Yet the garrison

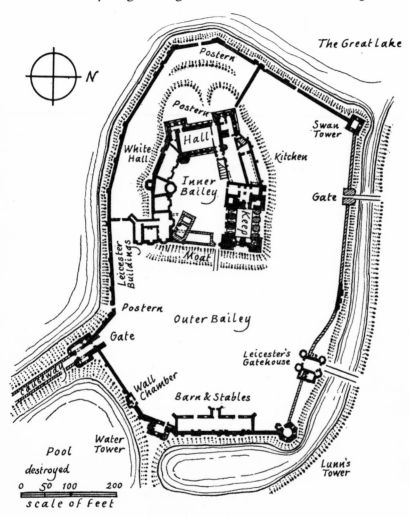

Plan of Kenilworth Castle

held out for six long months, and capitulated only under the compulsion of disease and famine. When the royal troops entered the castle they were almost overpowered by the stench of rotting bodies of men

5 *Kenilworth Castle*

and beasts. Thereafter Kenilworth was attached to the Duchy of Lancaster; and in the next century it became a favourite seat of John of Gaunt, by whom the castle was enlarged and reconstructed upon a magnificent scale. In 1563 Queen Elizabeth bestowed it upon her favourite, Robert Dudley, Earl of Leicester, whom she visited frequently at Kenilworth—notably in July 1575, when Leicester entertained the Queen and Court for seventeen days with a lavishness that astounded even Elizabethan England. Needless to say, the Earl added largely to the buildings of the castle. In the Civil War it was held by Parliament; nevertheless, in 1649, after their victory over the King, Cromwell's government decided to 'slight it', as the phrase went— that is, to dismantle the defences, but 'with as little spoil to the dwelling house as might be'. One half of the keep was blown up, and breaches blown in the curtain walls and flanking towers. The great dam was likewise breached, and the water in the lake was thus run off. Only Leicester's gatehouse continued to be occupied. In 1937 the owner, Lord Kenilworth, handed over the castle to the custody of the then Office of Works, coupling the gift with a handsome contribution towards the cost of putting the vast ruin into repair.

Three constituent elements have at various periods striven for dominance in the castle theme. These are, in the order of their emergence, the hall-house, the tower-house, and the gatehouse. The hall-house in its most primitive form was the timber *aula* of the earliest English settlers upon British soil—the old Germanic *Einraumhaus* which, serving all the domestic and festal requirements of a chief, furthermore with its great bulk and imposing high-pitched roof, portrayed his social eminence amid the log cabins or wattled huts of his dependents clustered around. Enclosed by a palisaded earthwork, such a timber hall-house formed the type of the manorial residences of those Teutonic chiefs who settled as conquerors upon the soil of the Western Empire.

With the break-up of the Carolingian Empire, the onset of the Norse invasions, and the rise of militant feudalism, accompanied by its distinctive scourge of private war, it came to pass that this early form of timber hall-house failed to afford sufficient protection to its owner. So, for security reasons, it was up-ended. The hall still remained in the centre, but instead of having the kitchen and offices at its lower end and the lord's private rooms at its upper end, the former were placed *beneath* the hall and the latter *above* it. Thus the hall-house became the tower-house. At first it was still made of timber, but for its better protection it was now set on top of a lofty earthen mound or *motte*. Later the tower-house itself was made of stone, and so arises the structure which in this country we know as a Norman keep. When such a stone keep was erected the earthen *motte* was omitted, since it was impossible to rear so ponderous a structure upon an artificial mound. If on the other hand a *motte* was already present, and it was desired to replace it by a stone building, the result is what is known as a 'shell-keep'.

Both the timber tower-house on its *motte* and the later stone keep had, of course, their bailey or appended base-court, containing the subsidiary buildings of the lord's household. In this disposition likewise, the development was from timber to stonework. The palisaded bank gives place to the masonry curtain wall. In this, a tower of entry or fortified gatehouse, of course, is requisite. And in the later Middle Ages the development of siegecraft and the rise of 'bastard feudalism' (see Chapter 10) led to the emergence of the gatehouse as the dominant element in the castle. It is remarkable how all these successive phases in the evolution of the English castle are illustrated in a single building at Kenilworth.

The great stone Norman keep still encloses within its basement the stump of the original *motte*, once crowned by its timber tower-house. In the same way, at Raglan Castle, the fifteenth century 'Yellow Tower of Gwent' encloses the core or stump of a Norman *motte* (see p. 159). At Kenilworth, the present inner ward represents the bailey of the early *motte*, and its ditch can still be traced.

The Norman keep itself nobly speaks for the second phase in this development, when the wooden tower-house came to be replaced in massive masonry. About the same time a stone curtain wall succeeded the palisaded rampart of the bailey. Much of it still remains, embodied in later work.

But in this great castle of Kenilworth there was also, from an early period, the wide outer bailey or basecourt; and here we can study the rise to importance of the gatehouse. Beginning in Norman times as a simple rectangular tower of entry, it was enlarged in the later thirteenth century into a powerful 'keep-gatehouse' of the Edwardian type (see Chapter 7).

Broadly speaking, a structure of this type represents the culminating stage in the evolution of the English castle. At Kenilworth, therefore, later development shifted the emphasis back from the gatehouse and away from the tower-house to the archetypal element of the hall-house. For John of Gaunt's buildings are nothing else than a hall-house on the most magnificent scale. Not only because of their splendour, but in the strict medieval use of the word we may describe them as 'palatial': for in the Latin of the Middle Ages palatium signifies a hall, and in old Scotch records a 'palace' or a 'house built palace-wise' is the regular name for a hall-house. In Germany, the word appears as *Palas or Pfalz*, the standard name for the hall in a castle, or for a castle devised on the hall-house plan.

In a castle new-built at the time of John of Gaunt, or in a major transformation of an existing castle, such as he carried out at Kenilworth, we should expect to find a self-contained suite of quarters for the military retainers of the lord's household. At Kenilworth there is no trace of any such provision. We can scarcely doubt that, as happened at Portchester Castle, and apparently also at Brough Castle in Westmorland, the old Norman keep was set aside for this purpose.

But this was not the end of the story at Kenilworth. In the final reorganisation, carried out by Dudley, noble expression was once again given to the gatehouse as a major element in the castle scheme. And, by a chance at once singular and significant, it is Leicester's Gatehouse that today remains the only inhabited portion of the whole vast and varied, many-dated complex of buildings that make up the Castle of Kenilworth.

When Colonel Hawkesworth, the Roundhead officer who had appropriated the castle, decided to make himself a residence therein, the Norman keep no longer lay to his hand. He had himself most effectively 'slighted' it. The residential buildings in the Inner Ward would be far too vast for his requirements; moreover they were doubtless much in disrepair. So he settled himself in Leicester's Gatehouse. Experience, as we shall learn in Chapter 7, had shown that the keep-gatehouses of Edwardian times did not make convenient residences. It was difficult to combine a dwelling house with a defended entry. So, in not a few cases a new entrance was provided elsewhere, and the passage of entry was walled up at both ends, so as to convert it into a cellar. Hence the gatehouse became a tower-house pure and simple. This was just what Colonel Hawkesworth did with Leicester's Gatehouse at Kenilworth. And, by so doing, he wrote the final chapter to an architectural history as remarkable as it is instructive. The wheel had come full circle. Leicester's Gatehouse, converted by the Puritan officer into a tower-house, became the residence of the lord of the manor, and though no longer used for this purpose, is still devoted to administrative purposes in connexion with the borough of Kenilworth.

A remarkable thing about the Kenilworth buildings is the sense of scenic architecture displayed in the work both of John of Gaunt and of Robert Dudley. On the west front of John of Gaunt's palace the Strong or Treasury Tower at the north end is balanced by a corresponding tower at the south end. This, however, is only make-belief. It is not arranged tower-wise internally, nor has it the thick walls, vaulted construction and small windows of the Treasury Tower. In the same way, a corresponding balance has been arranged in the Elizabethan remodelling, where Leicester's Building corresponds to the keep, with the low range of Henry VIII's work in between.

It is noteworthy that in his remodelling the Earl of Leicester retained in full use the great Norman keep, slapping out large Tudor windows in it. His contemporary Sir Christopher Hatton did the same with his keep at Corfe. Clearly there was no question of the Norman keep being an out-of-date feature in the Elizabethan reorganisation of both castles. But what purpose was it intended now to serve? In the next century, Lady Anne Clifford did just the same thing when restoring her castles of Brough and Brougham in Westmorland; and we know that in both she made the old Norman keep her residence. I have little doubt that at Kenilworth Leicester did likewise. In all these cases, I feel we must seek the motive in a spirit of deliberate antiquarianism, prompted by that pride in her past which was so characteristic of Elizabethan England, and finds perhaps its noblest expression in Shakespeare's historical plays. A Norman keep, even if gutted and refitted in Tudor fashion, remained a thing poles asunder from Elizabethan notions of house-planning. Yet it connected the present owner with an illustrious past upon which clearly he set much value. And if, as may well have been the case, Lord Leicester did indeed believe that the keep was 'Caesar's Tower', built by the Roman conqueror of Britain, he was surely anxious to preserve, as the leading feature of the castle he was so sumptuously rehabilitating, a building that linked imperial Rome with the new imperial Britain over which his royal mistress presided with a splendour that matched even that of the mighty Julius himself.

Finally a word must be said about the water defences of Kenilworth. A mighty dam, affording a broad causeway across the water to a large outer barbican, was constructed by the Norman engineers, so as to pond back the currents of two streams, flowing respectively past the south and west sides of the raised platform upon which the castle stands. In this way a lake or mere was formed, covering more than 100 acres. The castle buildings themselves, it may be added, include an area of no less than nine acres.

In addition to the immense architectural interest attached to Kenilworth Castle, and the great events that it has witnessed, the ruins are invested with a literary glamour almost unparalleled in England. The brilliant scenes of pageantry, intrigue, love, mystery and woe in which the castle figures in Scott's novel have cast around it an immortal glow. But we must not forget three other scenes, historically connected with the castle, which poetic genius has enshrined in imperishable verse. The tragic scene of Edward II's downfall, set forth in so piteous a manner in Marlowe's play, and the shameful incident, just outside the castle, in which the poor king's jailors shaved him in puddle water, likewise portrayed by the poet with heartrending intensity, are memorable episodes in one of the greatest of Elizabethan tragedies. And the famous incident in which Henry V received the French ambassadors with their mocking gift of tennis balls, so brilliantly dramatised in Shakespeare's play, took place at Kenilworth, doubtless in John of Gaunt's Hall—though the poet transfers the event to London.

WARWICK CASTLE, the other great palace-fortress of the Midlands, has come down to our own day not, like Kenilworth, as a shattered ruin, but intact and, though much altered in the seventeenth century and later, survives in its main Gothic features; so that it now stands as perhaps the most perfect example of a medieval castle of the first rank in all the length and breadth of England. It was a foundation in 1068 of William the Conqueror, and his great *motte*, crowned by the ruins of a shell-keep now much obscured by seventeenth-century embellishments, remains as a conspicuous feature at the north-west corner of the castle—just as at Caldicot; and, like Caldicot, the oblong bailey, doubtless extended in later times, stretches away to the east. The early castle is said to have been demolished in 1264 by de Montfort's partisans, 'who beat down the wall from tower to tower'; and certainly, with the exception of the shell-keep, the existing medieval work belongs mainly to the fourteenth century. It is in fact the product of a comprehensive reconstruction begun by Thomas Beauchamp, Earl of Warwick, who died in 1369, as a result of a disease contracted in the Hundred Years' War. The work which he left unfinished was completed in 1394 by his son. In the fifteenth century the Beauchamps were succeeded as Earls of Warwick by the Nevilles, of whom the most famous was the 'King Maker'. Notwithstanding the tremendous part which he played in the Wars of the Roses, his castle is not recorded to have suffered damage in that protracted strife. Indeed, for a building so situated and of such importance, its history has been surprisingly uneventful. In the early seventeenth century the interior of the habitable portions was much altered by Sir Fulk Greville, to whom the castle was granted by James I. During the Civil War it was held for Parliament, and stood a siege, which seems to have amounted to little more than an ineffective cannonade, at the hands of the Royalists.

The Jacobean and later splendours of the Warwick Castle interiors, familiar as they are to countless visitors, do not concern us here. Our business is with the fourteenth-century walls and towers, and the great hall of the same period. The castle fronts towards the north-east. Here there is an imposing gatehouse, elaborately defended, and still further protected by an external barbican. At either end of this front are the two massive and lofty towers which are the glory of Warwick. Indeed there is nothing finer of their kind and period in all England. Caesar's Tower on the left is an astonishing structure. Trilobed in plan, like a clover-leaf, and vaulted upon five of its six storeys, it rises to a height of no less than 133 feet. Its special feature is the double parapet, a lower one resting on bold machicolated corbels, within which rises an inner cylinder crowned by a flat roof behind a plain embrasured bartisan. Such a *double couronnement* is characteristically French: it forms a notable feature in the Château de Pierrefonds, where the splendid restoration by Viollet-le-Duc is, in this particular, fully justified not only by the surviving remains which he found, but also by old engravings.

Guy's Tower, 128 feet in height, which terminates the right of the entrance front, is polygonal in plan, likewise vaulted in all its five storeys; but it possesses only a single machicolated parapet.

On the north-east front of the castle a large four-square building with round angle towers is placed athwart the curtain. Begun but not finished by Richard III, this structure was designed for artillery. The present entrance through it appears to be comparatively modern.

The long south-east front of Warwick Castle, pierced by the numerous Gothic windows which light the 'palace' or living apartments, rising sheer above the River Avon, protected against the water by a massive stone 'apron', and terminated to the right by Caesar's Tower, is a sight which, once seen, can never be forgotten. Somewhat remarkably, the great hall is on a small scale for so palatial a residence: it measures only 62 feet by 42 feet. The hall was badly damaged by a fire in 1871, and the interior has been much modernised.

All in all, Macaulay was not far wrong in claiming Warwick Castle as 'the finest of those fortresses of the Middle Ages which have been turned into peaceful dwellings'. But in addition to all the many claims upon our attention, which I have no more than indicated in the foregoing sketch, the castle is invested in the glamour attaching to the medieval romance, *Guy of Warwick*. This famous poem describes the adventures of the mythical hero, who is said to have married the daughter and heiress of Roalt, Earl of Warwick. Remorse for the violence of his youth drives him to desert his wife and all her wealth, and to undertake a pilgrimage to the Holy Land. All manner of fantastic adventures, including combats with giants, dragons and monsters, beset his subsequent career, until at last he retires anonymously to a hermitage in the Forest of Arden, revealing his identity only on his deathbed. It is from him that Guy's Tower derives its name.

At Hever we considered a small medieval castle which has been reconditioned, embellished and filled with lovely treasures by the wealth and taste of a modern owner. At Warwick, on a far vaster scale, we have a similar reconstitution, but this took place in the reign of James I. From that time onwards, in the splendid state apartments erected by Sir Fulk Greville, and still further enhanced in the eighteenth century, treasures of all kinds have accumulated: priceless pictures, including historical portraits; tapestries, carpets, furniture, chandeliers, armour and weapons, silver plate and china ware. The spacious grounds were in part designed by 'Capability Brown' and complete the picture of a demesne and palace which Sir Walter Scott rightly describes as 'that fairest monument of ancient and chivalrous splendour which yet remains uninjured by time'.

3

Norman Castles of Timbered Earthwork

We have seen that the earliest castles thrown up in England by the conquering Normans were usually constructed not of stone and lime but of timbered earthwork; also that contemporary pictures of them may be studied in the Bayeux Tapestry. Contemporary descriptions have also survived, as in the famous portrayal of such a castle by a twelfth-century French writer. It has been translated thus:

> It was customary for the rich men and nobles of those parts, because their chief occupation is the carrying on of feuds and slaughters, in order that they may in this way be safe from enemies, and may have the greater power for either conquering their equals or keeping down their inferiors, to heap up a mound of earth as high as they were able, and to dig round it a broad, open and deep ditch, and to girdle the whole upper edge of the mound, instead of a wall, with a barrier of wooden planks, stoutly fixed together with numerous turrets set round. Within was constructed a house or rather citadel, commanding the whole, so that the gate of entry could only be approached by a bridge which, first springing from the counterscarp of the ditch, was gradually raised as it advanced, supported by sets of piers, two or even three, trussed on each side over convenient spans, crossing the ditch with a managed ascent so as to reach the upper level of the mound, landing at its edge on a level at the threshold of the gate.

Since the last war careful excavation has taught us much about the long vanished superstructures of our Norman mottes, mainly by recovering the post holes and sleeper beds. A curious fact revealed by such investigations is that these timber towers were sometimes reared upon posts, quite in the fashion of modern tower-blocks of flats by which our cities all over the world are progressively being reduced to a dead-pan uniformity of aspect—to the sad erosion of traditional and national styles of building. Many of these Norman wooden towers were of small dimensions: but always they were lofty, and nothing can be more absurd than certain modern drawings, purporting to be 'reconstructions', in which the *motte* is depicted as crowned by a thing like a rabbit-hutch.

One of the most impressive examples of Norman earthwork in Britain is to be found at PLESHEY in Essex. Here, carved out of stiff boulder-clay, we have a *motte* and bailey castle on a grand scale, to which is attached the bank and ditch of a borough, built to house the soldier burgesses whom the great Norman family of de Mandeville brought thither when they obtained a licence to build the castle from Henry II. William de Mandeville, grantee of the licence, was married at Pleshey in 1180, by which time it may be assumed that his castle was substantially complete. This view is confirmed by the result of excavations conducted in 1959, and fully reported by the Essex Archaeological Society with a promptness that might well serve as an example to the promoters of similar undertakings. Reference has already been made to Thomas of Woodstock, Duke of Gloucester, as the owner of Caldicot Castle, and to his murder at Calais in 1397 by order of his nephew, Richard II. The great Duke was also lord of Pleshey; and it was here that he was arrested by the King, who marched from London under cover of night, seized his uncle, and shipped him off to his secret death in Calais. Pleshey Castle was forfeited to the Crown, and its contents carried off for King Richard's use. Among the furniture noted in the inventory was the murdered Duke's 'great bed of gold, that is to say a coverlet, a tester, and the entire *celure* of fine blue satin wrought with garters of gold, and three curtains of *tartaryn* beaten to match; also two long and four square pillows of the set of the bed'. Shakespeare was probably not far wide of the mark when in *Richard II* he makes the widowed Duchess lament that at Pleshey Castle there remained naught

But empty lodgings and unfurnished walls,
Unpeopled offices, untrodden stones.

The Duchess appears to have been allowed to live on at Pleshey until she died in the same year that King Richard in his turn was murdered. The later history of the castle need not detain us long here. In 1450–60 it was occupied by Henry VI's formidable Queen, Margaret of Anjou, when important building was done in the new fashionable material of brick; but by the time of Queen Elizabeth's accession Pleshey Castle had become a total ruin: the *motte*, we are told, was then 'replenyshed with coneyes'.

The whole area of town and castle comprises about $11\frac{1}{2}$ acres. The town lies to the north of the castle, and is dominated by the latter's *motte*, while the kidney-shaped bailey adjoins the *motte* on the south. Sixty feet in height, the *motte* is surrounded by a wide and deep wet ditch, still full of water. Inside the ditch the rampart of the bailey is 18 feet in height above ground level. The original entrance to the bailey was on the north-east side. It seems to have been constructed as a timber bridge of two spans, resting on an 'island'. After crossing this bridge, almost the whole of the inner margin of the bailey had to be traversed before the steep causeway leading up to the *motte* was reached. Thus a hostile party would present their right sides, unprotected by their shields, to the defenders high above them on the *motte*. In the fifteenth century the causeway up the *motte* was replaced by a brick bridge of a single arch. This is now the only masonwork bulking large upon the site; but the foundations of a hall-house were found on top of the *motte* during excavations carried out in 1907, when also stone buildings were uncovered in the bailey. Here many glazed flooring tiles were found. Town ditch and bank still survive in good condition, and the *ensemble* presents us with an impressive example of Norman military engineering. Within the town was the twelfth-century parish church of the Holy Trinity: but in the fifteenth century this was replaced by a collegiate establishment outside the ramparts. This was in accordance with a common practice, of which we shall meet with other examples.

The site of Pleshey was occupied in Roman times, and, both in the village and in the long interrupted trench dug in 1959 within the bailey, coins dating from the late third century have been recovered. In the trench the post-poles and sleeper-slots of Norman timber buildings, as well as stone foundations and cobbling of a late date, were met with. The Norman buildings had been thatched. A large assemblage of finds was collected, including coins of Edward I; potsherds ranging from the twelfth to the sixteenth century; bronze pins and tweezers; iron knives, gouges, horseshoes and arrow-heads; bottle glass, coloured window-glass; roof and floor tiles; and so forth. A singular find was a fourteenth-century chimney pot. The abundance of relics recovered in five weeks' digging shows that Pleshey Castle is indeed a rich site. On every ground it is to be hoped that the excavations, so ably begun, will in due course be continued.

The site of DUDLEY CASTLE, Staffordshire, is one of noble majesty. It crowns the highest point of a long Silurian limestone hill, rising from 120 to 150 feet above the adjoining level, having the town of Dudley extending over a ridge which prolongs the castle site towards the south, while northward is spread a broad expanse of plainland, once a smiling agricultural and forest country, and even now wonderfully beautiful in spite of all that coal and iron have done to mar its countenance. The actual site of the castle has been organised by banking and ditching into a mount and bailey plan. Oval in shape, the bailey measures about 340 feet in length from north to south, and 265 feet in greatest breadth. It is enclosed by a formidable ditch quarried in the limestone, outside which is a substantial counterscarp mound. The mount is at the south-west corner, dominating the town. For the most part the timber defences of mount and bailey seem to have remained in use until the fourteenth century. But a Norman gatehouse is embodied in the present gatehouse and barbican, a composite structure of Edwardian date; and there certainly were Norman domestic buildings of stone, for one or two fragments still survive in the Plantagenet and Tudor edifices that have replaced them. A licence to crenellate in stone and lime was issued for Dudley in 1263, but it seems clear that the existing curtain wall and the tower-house are not earlier than the fourteenth century.

Of Sir John de Somery, who held the lordship of Dudley from 1300 to 1321, we are fortunate in having a distinct account. In a complaint dated 1311, it is stated that

> he has obtained such mastery in the country of Stafford that no one can obtain law or justice therein; that he has made himself more than a king there; that no one can dwell there unless he buys protection from him

either by money or by assisting him in building his castles, and that he attacks people in their own houses with the intention of killing them unless they make fine for his protection.

Here then we have the authentic portrait of a baronial thug, of the type that was to become increasingly common in the fourteenth and fifteenth centuries. In Sir John de Somery's case we see that what Mr Trevelyan calls the 'revival of anarchy in a civilised society', usually regarded as a consequence of the Hundred Years' War, had already made itself grimly apparent during the weak government of Edward II—as a result, no doubt, of the exhaustion and demoralisation caused by the long effort to subdue Scotland. Truly Plantagenet imperialism was putting forth evil fruits. Sir John de Somery, terrorising a countryside with his armed hirelings, was the very man to build himself, for his mere safety, a self-contained tower-house in which, within his own castle, he could dwell apart from the garrison of cut-throats that he maintained to enforce his will upon the victims of his nefarious schemes.

His tower-house is a most remarkable structure, and its partial demolition in the Civil War is much to be regretted. Crowning the Norman *motte*, it is oblong on plan, with stout half-round or drum towers at the corners. The entrance was defended by a portcullis, and the walls are provided with an embattled parapet. As Sir Harold Brak-spear well remarks,

> the whole arrangement of this keep was of a small manor-house; the hall on the first floor with two chambers at the west end, the screens at the east end with the pantry and buttery in the eastern drums, and a serving stair to the ground floor, which was probably used for kitchen and servants' quarters.

About the same time when the tower-house was built on the mount, the bailey was massively walled in, and along its eastern side a complete set of domestic apartments was erected, the old Norman buildings in the progress being almost swept away. The new buildings comprised the usual accommodation of kitchen, hall, great chamber and chapel, with ample cellarage and offices. The fact that these buildings were erected at the same time as the tower-house clearly brings out the significance of the latter as a residence set apart for the lord and his family, into which they could, if they wished, withdraw themselves from the rest of his unruly household. This is a radically different state of affairs from what took place when a twelfth-century keep fell into disuse and was replaced by domestic buildings in the courtyard.

These courtyard buildings at Dudley were twice remodelled in Tudor times. The earlier refashioning was carried out in the reign of Edward VI for the Duke of Northumberland under the direction of Sir William Sharington, a pioneer of the earliest or Italianate phase of the English Renaissance. Elsewhere I have suggested that Sharington's architect, both for his own works at Lacock Abbey and for the magnificent conversion that he carried out for his ducal patron at Dudley, was John Shute, author of the *First and Chief Groundes of Architecture*, published in 1563, who in 1550 made a journey to Italy at the Duke's expense in order to study the buildings of the Italian Renaissance.[1]

In 1644 the Castle successfully withstood a three-weeks' siege by the Roundheads, but on 10 May, 1645, it surrendered to Sir William Brereton, and next year the donjon and curtain walls were partly demolished, so as to render the place untenable. The domestic buildings, however, continued to be inhabited until in 1750 they were gutted in a three days' fire (24-26 July). It is said that the blaze was occasioned by the illicit activities of a gang of coiners. That it may have been premeditated is suggested by a sinister inscription, formerly to be seen at the kitchen door, as if left uncompleted by a prospective incendiary:

> Water went rond it, to garde it from the Fooe,
> The fire shall burn it . . .

In modern times the vast Norman earthworks of Dudley Castle have been fitted up as a zoo, now containing one of the finest collections of wild animals to be found in Britain elsewhere than at Whipsnade. Thus the twelfth-century banks and ditches have sprung into life once again in a way assuredly never contemplated by their creators. Thousands who come to see the zoo stay on to explore the remains of one of the noblest of English castles. When one sees an elephant, laden with delighted children, pacing sedately through the Norman courtyard, the words of a German poet occur to the mind—through not perhaps quite in the way intended by the author:

> *Das Alte stürtzt, es ändert sich die Zeiten*
> *Und neues Leben blüht aus den Ruinen!*

[1] For Dudley Castle reference may be made to my two papers in *The Archaeological Journal*, vol. XCV, pp. 142–58, and vol. CI, pp. 119–25.

With Dudley Castle we must consider WARKWORTH, that proud strong-hold of the Percies in Northumberland. Not without good reason, Professor Hamilton Thomson has described this as 'the most instructive of English castles'. Like Dudley, it began, in the hands of its first recorded owners, Earls of Northumberland of the Scottish royal line, as a mount and bailey castle on a very large scale. Its site is a remarkable one, in a great loop of the River Coquet, which, here flowing betwixt steep wooded banks, encloses the area on west, north and east. On such an *assiette* the natural thing would be to place the castle in the extreme angle of the promontory. But at Warkworth it is the town that occupies this ground, and the castle lies in front of it, in the open throat of the loop, facing out to what in olden days was the moorland country south-ward. Partly this will be due to the fact that the castle site is the highest ground, from which the area occupied by the little borough falls away northward, until it becomes a haugh by the riverside. Partly also the explanation may be that there was already an Anglo-Saxon township in the Coquet long before the Norman castle was founded. The mount and bailey lay-out conforms to the common pattern, the bailey having the shovel-shaped outline so commonly found in England. We get a clear though brief description of the castle in its earliest form on the occasion of its capture by the Scots in 1173, when it is described as 'feeble in wall and earthwork'. Warkworth then belonged to the Claverings, who held the barony until 1332. Under this powerful Norman family the timbered earthwork defences were, by successive stages, replaced in stone. A massive, ashlar-faced curtain, fully equipped with flanking defences, and provided with a formidable gatehouse, replaced the early palisading; and a domestic range, conceived on a great scale, was built along the inside of the west curtain. The flanking tower known as the 'Grey Mare's Tail' is famous for its giant cross-bow loopholes, 16 feet long, with 'plunged' fan-tail bases. These are the largest of this kind in England. On top of the *motte* a stone keep was erected, of which some fragments remain in the present extra-ordinary tower-house.

Upon the failure of the Clavering line Edward III granted Wark-worth to Sir Henry Percy, as part payment for the expenses which he had incurred in defending the eastern march against the Scots. As the Percies found it, the castle was the product of what we may describe as a process of aggrandisement of the bailey against the *motte*. Whatever may have been the condition of the donjon upon the *motte*, it seems clear that latterly the whole emphasis of the castle was concentrated on the well-defended bailey with its elaborate and beautiful domestic buildings. But with the coming of the Percies, the stress was shifted back from the bailey to the *motte*; and the latter was crowned by the imposing tower-house which is the glory of Warkworth. Containing within its own walls a complete suite of public and private apartments, this astonishing structure must at once have superseded the domestic range in the bailey, which no doubt, as at Dudley, was henceforth intended to be assigned to the lord's retainers, in a frontier castle the defence of which was a matter of national importance.

Heraldic evidence makes it clear that the tower-house was built not later than about 1390. Its shape is an extraordinary one. It may be regarded as a square with canted angles, from the middle of each side of which projects a small square, likewise having its angles canted. Within this bizarre outline, we find a well articulated house proper to an owner of the first rank. The internal arrangement is grouped round a central lantern which rises through the entire height of the tower-house, supplying borrowed light to the inner rooms and passages, as well as providing for roof drainage—the rain water being stored in a large stone tank in the basement, from which by a system of conduits the latrine shafts were flushed. In the basement are vaulted cellars and a prison, with an inner cell, as well as a darksome 'pit' below. On the first floor are the hall, kitchen, great chamber and chapel, all provided with ample windows. The hall, kitchen and chapel all rise through two storeys, while over the great chamber is a withdrawing room or parlour. In the nave of the chapel there was an oriole or gallery. The tower-house had a flat embattled roof, with a high square watch turret rising in the centre. So bald an outline of the accommodation in the building will give little idea of the intricate ingenuity of its design. Throughout, the masonry is of the finest ashlar, and the decorative detail is at once vigorous and restrained. On the face towards the borough, in high relief and on a large scale, is sculptured the lion rampant of the Percies— proud emblem of a prideful race. 'This lion holds up the castle', quoth James I when he visited Warkworth in 1617.

In the later medieval period, a great lord who wished to reorganise his capital seat upon up-to-date lies, and to provide therein an establishment which should adequately portray his own magnificence, would

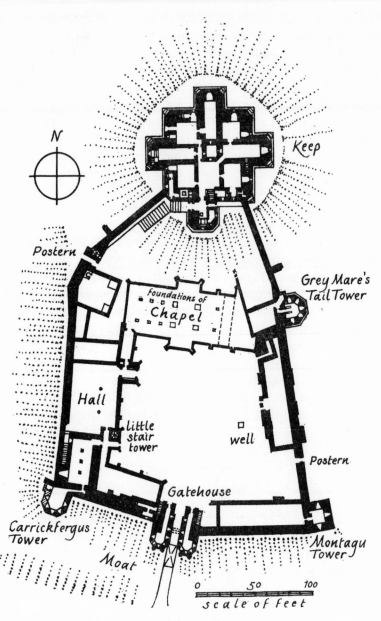

N

Keep

Postern

Grey Mare's
Tail Tower

foundations of
Chapel

Hall

little
stair
tower

well

Postern

Gatehouse

Carrickfergus
Tower

Montagu
Tower

Moat

0   50   100
scale of feet

Plan of Warkworth Castle

not rest content with refashioning his castle in splendid style. I have already spoken of the feudal connexion between parish church and castle, as the ecclesiastical and civil *nuclei* respectively of the manorial organism. But in this ancient association the castle had long outstripped its ecclesiastical neighbour. While the baronage in the thirteenth and fourteenth centuries were incessantly remodelling their residences and enhancing their grandeur, their generosity towards Holy Church took the form rather of endowing monasteries or subscribing towards the rebuilding or enlargement of cathedrals. But in the last century of the Middle Ages the baron steps in again to restore his credit as a patron of local church building. No longer does he figure as a benefactor of cathedrals or monasteries. There are more than enough of these lazy monks already, he thinks, and those proud prelates have waxed over rich through the mistimed generosity of his ancestors. So our baron now finds an outlet for his piety in the new fashion of founding a collegiate church, served by a master or provost and chaplain, in the immediate neighbourhood of his castle. Such a corporation, by its very proximity, was more intimately bound to pray for the founder's soul and family than the monks in their distant abbey or the chantry priests in their cathedral. Thus the connexion between these new collegiate foundations and the manorial centre was a close one, physically no less than institutionally. We have already noted the new practice at Pleshey, and shall come across further examples in the following pages. In one or two notable cases, the collegiate church was erected within the castle walls of its founder. The grandest example of this, of course, is St George's Chapel at Windsor. At Warkworth the foundations of such a collegiate establishment, never finished, bestraddle the castle courtyard. It was designed as a cruciform church, with aisles in nave and chancel and a central tower. What moulded detail survives suggests a date about contemporary with the tower-house; and a sixteenth-century writer tells us that the college was interposed as a division between the lodgings around the courtyard and the lord's residence in the tower-house—thus providing additional seclusion for the latter from the armed retainers to whom we must presume that the courtyard lodgings were now abandoned.

The history of Warkworth Castle is writ large in the annals of border warfare. Captured by the Scots in 1173, in 1327 it was twice successfully held against them. During the Percy rebellion of 1405 against

Henry IV, the castle was battered into surrender by the royal artillery. In 1644 it yielded to the Army of the Covenant. By that time the interior buildings were in sore disrepair. Shakespeare in *King Henry IV* describes it as a 'worm-eaten hold of ragged stone'; and this we know to have been its condition in the dramatist's time, however inapposite the description is for the reign of the first Lancastrian monarch—when indeed the castle was at the very height of its puissance and glory.

The small fragments of the early donjon at Warkworth, embodied in the later tower-house, are badly dislocated, evidently through a failure in its foundations. Such a thing was apt to happen when a heavy stone building was imposed upon an artificial *motte*. Of this a spectacular example is furnished by the donjon at the royal castle of YORK.

Eboracum, for so the Romans called it, was the military capital of *Britannia*, as *Londinium* was the commercial metropolis. Few scholars now doubt that York, like London, maintained its existence, however enfeebled, as a civic centre throughout the so-called 'Dark Ages', until in the early seventh century, *Eoforwic* emerges again as the civil and ecclesiastical capital of the Anglian kingdom of Northumbria. Always it had been a military base against enemies to the north: under the Romans against the Picts, and in post-Roman times against the emergent and aggressive kingdom of Scotland. Its strong sense of independence, inherited from the proud Northumbrian kingdom, made it a focus of disaffection against the rule of the Norman conqueror. It is therefore not surprising that William I threw up, not one but two large *mottes* to bridle the unruly city and to secure his northern border against the Scots. One of these *mottes*, with its bailey attached, still remains on the opposite bank of the River Ouse from the Roman city. The other, to the south of the latter, became one of the finest examples of a mount and bailey in northern England. In the mid-thirteenth century the timber superstructure of the *motte* was replaced by the most remarkable stone keep of that period in Britain. It has long been known as Clifford's Tower, apparently from the fact that over its parapet was hung in chains the body of Roger de Clifford, one of the rebel barons defeated by Edward II at Boroughbridge in 1322. Building records show that the work was begun in 1245; and by the end of Henry III's reign (1272), almost £2000, an enormous sum in those days, had been spent on the keep and on the stone walls and towers of the bailey. The work was entrusted by the King to the royal master mason, Henry of Reynes—no less a person than the great architect to whom we owe the thirteenth-century work at Westminster Abbey. Confirmation of this exciting fact is found in the presence, as a loose fragment found during the excavations at Clifford's Tower, of a most lovely corbel-cap portraying the head of a Queen, unmistakably a product of the high Westminster school of figure sculpture.[1]

Clifford's Tower is built in the shape of a quatrefoil. Only one other example of this peculiar design is known to have existed in England, namely the keep of Pontefract Castle, also in Yorkshire. In all probability the prototype is to be sought in the well known French donjons at Étampes and Amblény. As might be expected in a work built by Master Henry the Mason, Clifford's Tower is a most finished piece of ashlar masonry. It rises from a broadly outspread plinth, and all the details are in the finest First Pointed Gothic. The arcading of the chapel, which occupies a small forework, is particularly rich. A remarkable feature is found in the ground floor windows, which take the form of rect-angular openings, with shouldered heads, while from the sill of each a long loophole, terminating in an oilette, is carried down well into the sloping plinth of the tower. The tower contained two unvaulted storeys of well-appointed living rooms; the floor between them, and doubtless the roof, were carried upon a central pier. It is likely that a third storey was contemplated. There are two mural stairs, and the tower contains a well, said to have been 60 feet deep.

Almost from the beginning difficulty seems to have been encountered in setting this ponderous tower upon an artificial mound. Before 1312 the chapel in the forework required reconstruction. In 1360 the tower is reported to be 'cracked from top to bottom in two places'. Today it is badly split, so that the walls are tilted outwards. Intricate works have had to be undertaken to prevent a total collapse. These include the underpinning of the southern sector by a concentric framework of concrete ribs, like the spokes of a wheel. This unique tower is now in the custody of the Ministry of Public Building and Works.

Considerable remains survive of the thirteenth-century stone curtain walls and towers, and on the north and west sides the outline of the

---

[1] See my book, *The Castle of Bergen and the Bishop's Palace at Kirkwall*, p. 49 and Fig. 15.

entire bailey is clearly defined in the existing street plan. On the other sides the boundary is the River Foss.

This history of York Castle is that of the city which for more than six centuries it dominated. In the Civil War it was held for King Charles, but yielded to the victorious Roundheads after their victory at Marston Moor in 1644. On 23 April 1684, the tower was gutted by a fire, in the course of a salute of guns to mark St George's Day. 'It was generally thought a wilful act,' so records a contemporary diarist, 'the soldiers not suffering the citizens to enter till it was too late; and what made it more suspicious was, the gunner had got out all his goods before it was discovered'.

We have seen at York that the Conqueror threw up two mount and bailey castles, one on either side of the Ouse, to bridle an unruly city— and also (we can hardly doubt) to control a navigable river against a Danish fleet, such as in 1069, which landed the army that captured York, including its two castles. By contrast, at LEWES in Sussex, one of the Conqueror's leading barons, William de Warenne, whom the King appointed his Chief Justiciar, built himself a castle with two *mottes*, one to command the valley of the Sussex Ouse, and the other to dominate the town. The principal *motte* is that towards the west: the eastern is known as Brack Mount. The mounds are wholly artificial, heaped up with large chunks of quarried chalk. Before the eleventh century was out, the palisades of the western mount and the bailey had been replaced by substantial walls of flint rubble, displaying in places the herringbone pattern of face work so often found in early Norman masonry (see p. 46). But no stone structure seems ever to have crowned Brack Mount. A single square gatehouse gave access from the town, and two other square mural towers still in part remain. For the dressed work of these buildings, limestone was brought across from Caen in Normandy.

Such, then, was the Norman castle of the Warrennes. Of the interior buildings no definite traces survive. Upon the bare slopes of the South Downs, close west of the town, Simon de Montfort, on 14 May 1264, gained his famous victory over the forces of Henry III—an event that had such momentous consequences in English constitutional history. In the street fighting that followed Earl Simon's triumph the town of

Lewes will have suffered severely, but there is no word of damage to the castle. Nevertheless, it seems probable that thereafter the two handsome multangular towers were added to the shell keep. They are unvaulted, but substantially built of large flints, with dressed quoin stones. A remarkable feature is the presence of loopholes or arrow-slits placed at the external angles of the towers. Both towers rise from bold

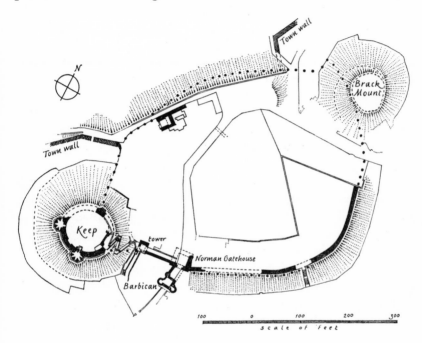

Plan of Lewes Castle

aprons or sloping bases, carried well down the side of the *motte*. The latest addition to the castle was made some time in the first half of the fourteenth century, when a handsome barbican was added in front of the Norman gateway on the curtain wall. Though somewhat restored, this barbican is one of the finest things of its kind in England. With its tall corbelled turrets, cruciform loopholes, and boldly machicolated parapet, it strongly reminds me of the 'bars' in the town walls of York. Of special interest is the masonry of knapped flints, small and closely packed.

The later history of Lewes Castle is uneventful. It was badly damaged in a riot of the burghers in 1382, and thereafter seems to have been abandoned to a slow decay. In 1620 its buildings were being pulled down for the sake of their materials. In 1774 the ruins were leased to a local wool merchant, who converted the keep into a summer house. Of his operations a handsome rusticated, pseudo-classical doorway, admitting to the western tower, and the round staircase of the eastern tower, are the principal survivals. The castle is now the property of the Sussex Archaeological Society.

'Now England breathes in the hope of liberty' cried an exultant poet after the battle of Lewes. No one nowadays regards 'Earl Simon the Righteous'—so the humble folk of England loved to call him—as a pure selfless patriot. Yet it is impossible, as one looks out over the battlefield of 1264 from the high turret of the castle, not to think with emotion of that famous day, which, if it did not result in the 'creation of the House of Commons', nevertheless was undoubtedly the victory that led directly to what a modern historian has termed 'the first occasion on which the rulers of England deliberately took the people into partnership with them'. Earl Simon's effort was bound to fail, since after all he was an alien and a rebel against his King, and overbearing and fractious besides. But the lesson of his astonishing career was not lost upon the young Prince Edward, the real commander of the royalists at Lewes; and in due course it was reserved for him, as the greatest of English kings, to vindicate the cause of 'good governance' and to make the English monarchy a truly national institution, and the real source of political progress.

One of the finest and best preserved examples of a large mount-and-bailey castle of normal pattern, later invested in stonework, is TICKHILL, on the southern border of Yorkshire. In certain early documents it is called the Castle of Blyth, from the more important place, with its Benedictine Priory, just over the Nottinghamshire border. In the same way, Corfe Castle in Purbeck is sometimes referred to as the Castle of Wareham. A Scottish parallel can be quoted from Banffshire, where Balvenie Castle appears in records of the War of Independence as the Castle of Mortlach, from the important early Christian centre close by. The Honour of Tickhill, a creation of the Conqueror, 'numbered sixty-five and three-quarters knights' fees, and extended from Yorkshire into

6   Warwick Castle from the west

the shires of Derby, Lincoln, Notts and Leicester, including one manor in Devon'. Of this noble demesne the grantee was Roger de Buisli, who made his chief residence at Tickhill. To him, therefore, the mighty earthworks must be assigned. It cannot have been long before the timber superstructures were replaced in masonry. Henry I appears in due course as lord of Tickhill. Under Henry II it was again Crown property. His Queen, Eleanor of Aquitaine, founded within the castle a chapel dedicated to St Nicholas, for which she generously endowed and provided a warden and four chaplains. During King Richard's absence on Crusade, the castle was seized by his treacherous brother, Prince John, but was besieged and captured by Hugh Pudsey, Bishop of Durham. King John was repeatedly at Tickhill, which he caused to be repaired. In 1208 five jars of red wine, 'such as will keep', were sent there for the royal table. In 1264 Henry III granted Tickhill to his son, Prince Edward, who settled it upon his wife, Eleanor of Castile. Under Edward II the castle was again Crown property, and in 1322 was attacked by his rebellious cousin, Thomas of Lancaster, who for three weeks battered it with stone-throwing engines, until the castle was relieved by the King in person.

We need not follow in detail the subsequent history of Tickhill. By Edward III it was given to his son John of Gaunt, in exchange for the Honour of Richmond. Its active history closed in the Civil War, when it was held for the King, surrendered to the Roundheads after Marston Moor, and subsequently dismantled.

A perfect cone in shape, the *motte* measures about 75 feet in height and 80 feet in summit diameter. The lower third of it is natural, and at least partly of red sandstone. It is enclosed by a deep ditch, with a broad counterscarp; but the segment within the bailey has long been filled in. The bailey, of an irregular oval form, is defended by a formidable ditch, much of which still retains its water, and affords an impressive example of this kind of Norman exterior defence. As late as the Civil War the counterscarp was palisaded. The whole area of these earthworks is almost 7 acres.

The oldest stonework appears to be in the gatehouse, erected about 1100. The curtain wall is on record in 1130-1, and the shell-keep on the mount was built by Henry II in 1178-80. With its round-arched portals in front and rear, the gatehouse is an interesting structure. Here, as throughout the castle, the Norman work is of grey stone, but in Tudor

7   *Clifford's Tower, York*

times the upper portion was partly rebuilt in red sandstone of squared rubble. Towards the courtyard it displays a handsome window in two compartments, each of two lights, all transomed. In the fourteenth century a low flat bridge was carried across the outer portal, so as to provide an extra overhead defence.

The bailey curtain is composed of various materials, obviously of different ages. Parts of it are faced with splendid ashlar, large square blocks regularly coursed and closely jointed. Other parts are in good coursed rubble, widely jointed. Externally the south curtain is buttressed. On the inside, a ragged mass of hearting is applied to this curtain, and ascends the mount, to which doubtless it carried a stair of access. Only foundations remain of the stone tower on the mount. It was decagonal, with angle-buttresses. Of the buildings within the bailey almost nothing survives, save a seventeenth-century armorial doorway, now built into the garden wall of the modern house. Its wooden door asks the pleasing prayer:

> Peace and grace
> Be in this place.

This important castle also provides us with an excellent example of the characteristic Norman context of parish church and manorial seat. The church, dedicated to St Mary, is a fine Perpendicular building, embodying earlier remnants. Its lofty tower, with an ornate parapet, is a landmark. The old black-and-white timbered hospital, now the church room, and the market cross, with other ancient buildings, complete the pleasant portrait of a manorial village that has grown up under the shelter of a great baronial stronghold. To enhance the picture, hard by are the ruins (now converted into a dwelling) of a Priory of Austin Canons, founded in 1276.

The ancient borough of TAMWORTH in Staffordshire has played its part in English history since Saxon times. In the eighth century it was the capital of Mercia, the midland kingdom of the so-called 'Heptarchy'; and here its most formidable King, Offa (787–96) had his palace, 'for its magnificence the admiration and wonder of the age', so we are assured by the Anglo-Saxon Chronicle. The ecclesiastical centre of the Mercian kings was fixed at Lichfield; and, here as elsewhere, we observe the wariness of our early kings in planting the seat of a supernatural and super-national power at some distance from the royal capital: compare Canterbury and London, York and Bamborough, Glasgow and Dumbarton, Iona and Dunadd. Its site has not so far been identified; but we are not to imagine the royal residence as in any way a primitive or barbaric structure. The Normans pulled down all the major buildings of Saxon England, and treated the architectural achievement of their predecessors with scorn: but modern research has taught us more justly to appreciate Anglo-Saxon architecture and art in all their varied manifestations, and to realise at last the stark fact that the Norman Conquest was an artistic catastrophe from which England did not fully recover until well on in the twelfth century. Tamworth is for ever associated with the illustrious name of Ethelfleda, 'Lady of Mercia', the heroic daughter of a hero king, who carried on the work of her father, Alfred the Great, in defending England from the Danes. The prongs of her multiple attack were the founding of fortified boroughs, banked and palisaded settlements, built 'for the protection of all the people', and as bases for advance against the Danelaw. One of these (founded in 913) was at Tamworth, meant to secure Mercia against a Danish attack based on Leicester. The memory of this splendid lady has been commemorated by a statuary group at the foot of the *motte* of Tamworth Castle, placed where it is (as an inscription records) on the assumption that this Norman work was 'Ethelfleda's mound'. She is shown with her left arm round the neck of her grandson, the future King Athelstan, while in her right hand she grasps a naked sword. At first sight, the effect produced is oddly reminiscent of Medea meditating the murder of her children! Doubtless at Tamworth, King Offa established a mint, and its earlier issues 'are distinguished by portraits showing a delicacy of execution which is unique in the whole history of the Anglo-Saxon coinage'.

William the Conqueror granted Tamworth to one of his companion adventurers, Robert de Marmion—a name rendered illustrious by Sir Walter Scott, though the family had long ceased to own Tamworth by the time of 'Flodden Field'. In the days of their pride the Marmions were 'Champions of England': that is to say, it was the privilege of Lord Marmion at a coronation to appear in arms and to declare his duty and determination to defend against all comers the king's claim to the

throne. If any person, of what degree soever, high or low, should deny
the king's right,

> here is his champion, who saith that he lieth, and is a false traitor, being
> ready in person to combat with him; and in this quarrel will adventure
> his life against him, on what day soever he shall be appointed.

By Robert de Marmion doubtless will have been thrown up the
mighty enditched *motte* that ever since has dominated Tamworth
town. Before the eleventh century was out, its summit had been crowned
by a massive polygonal curtain of red sandstone rubble, with a wing-
wall descending the slope to connect with the borough, which seems
to have served as a bailey. This wing-wall provides us with one of the
finest examples of herringbone masonry, a feature characteristic of
Norman work before about the year 1100. Flat stones are selected, and
each succeeding course is sloped in a direction contary to that of the
course below. To secure a firm bed above the uptilted edges, a horizontal row of spalls, or small stones, is introduced. In the twelfth
century a square tower was added, partly projecting from the curtain,
and so placed as to command the stair on the wing-wall by which the
motte was ascended from the town. By later owners of Tamworth, the
interior of the shell-keep was crowded with picturesque buildings,
partly stone and partly brick, in such a way as to leave only a small
courtyard, irregular and gloomy. Most of these buildings, which include
a fine Tudor hall, with an open-timbered roof, belong to the sixteenth,
seventeenth and eighteenth centuries. They have in part been used to
house an excellent local museum by the City Corporation, who now
own the castle. From the reign of Athelstan to that of Henry I there
was a royal mint at Tamworth; and the most interesting feature in the
museum is the undoubtedly fine collection of coins struck there, in
many cases stamped with the name of the moneyer. Tamworth Castle
now stands in a charming pleasance, and the whole presentation of the
venerable building and its surroundings reflects the utmost credit upon
the municipal authorities.

In this chapter I have tried briefly to describe a number of Norman
castles which began as timbered earthworks, and in each case to offer a
sketch of its history. Several others have been or will be encountered

elsewhere in this book. But in the total no more than a few will be mentioned among the numerous examples of this type of structure still to be found in almost all parts of England and Wales. Foremost among those which I have left aside is the largest of all, royal Windsor, which, after more than seven centuries of building and rebuilding, still retains the grand outlines of its Norman predecessor, remarkable for its double bailey, extending like gigantic wings on either side of the *motte*, and containing in its western bailey one of the noblest of English shrines, the sumptuous Chapel of St George, founded by Edward IV for the Knights of the Garter.[1] The same double-bailey plan is found at Arundel Castle in Sussex, the magnificent palace of the Duke of Norfolk, hereditary Marshal of England. At Durham, the characteristic Norman association of church and castle is displayed in imperial fashion, where the church is one of the grandest of European cathedrals, and the castle is the palace of a prince-bishop. The castle, which now houses the kernel of Durham University, still reveals in the outline of its stone buildings the mount and bailey upon which these have been built; and the *ensemble* of cathedral and palace, as seen from the railway, is without its like in Britain. The great Border castle of Norham, likewise a palatine fortress of the Bishops of Durham, began its tremendous history as a large *motte* and bailey: here the *motte* appears to be natural in substance, because upon it later was imposed one of the finest of Norman stone towers. Gladly also would I have written something about Berkeley in Gloucestershire, one of the noblest of our Norman castles which can boast uninterrupted occupation. Its proud history has been distorted, in popular imagination, by the murder within its walls of Edward II, under circumstances so revolting that even Marlowe, that artist in horror, flinched from presenting the full enormity of the scene upon his stage. In Cornwall, besides the ring-castle of Restormel (see pp. 48-51), we find an interesting group of mount-and-bailey castles of more normal type:—Taunton, Totnes, and Launceston, all with their *mottes* later provided with shell-keeps, and Launceston in addition exhibiting proudly a round tower within its shell-wall. In Wales, we may mention Cardiff, one of the most remarkable archaeological sites in Britain. Here the stone curtain walls follow the outline of a late Roman coastal fort, and the Roman north gate has been brilliantly restored.

[1] For Windsor Castle, see my *Exploring Castles*, Chapter IX.

Within the enclosure is the Norman *motte* crowned by its shell-keep. The castle was founded about 1090 by Robert Fitzhamon.

Everywhere in the British Islands, where the Normans have settled, their characteristic earthworks, often later invested in stone, remain to witness the former presence of the great master-race of medieval Europe. Most of these castles are on record in history; but, in England certainly, there are a large number of *mottes* about which history is silent. They are unpedigreed and anonymous. It is thought that many of these may be the so-called 'adulterine' castles, which were thrown up without royal licence during the anarchy under King Stephen, when it is said that no less than 1,117 of these unlicenced castles were built in England. Most of these would be destroyed when order was restored under the strong rule of Henry II.

Sometimes it befell that Norman military engineers threw up or carved out for themselves a mount so large that all the buildings of the lord's household could be included within its palisaded cincture or stone curtain wall. In such cases no bailey would be required. Castles of this type are better described as 'ring castles' rather than as *mottes*. Perhaps the most impressive example is to be found at RESTORMEL, near Lostwithiel in Cornwall. Certainly this is the most interesting and attractive castle in the Duchy. The enclosure forms an almost perfect circle, about 125 feet in overall diameter. In its earliest state the defences will have been, as usual, of palisading. About the year 1100 their replacement in stone began with the building of a square projecting gatehouse on the south-western sector. Early in the thirteenth century the palisade was replaced with a stout ring wall, still in perfect preservation, including the battlements, which are reached by a stair curving upwards from a first floor window. Up to this time, or later, it would appear that the interior buildings on top of the mound continued to be of timber. But about the end of the thirteenth century, no doubt by Edmund, Earl of Cornwall (1272–99), these were replaced by a well-articulated and handsome suite of apartments extending all round the interior of the curtain. A square tower was built out on the east side, containing a chapel above a vaulted undercroft, with a timber lodging for the priest set against the exterior of the curtain wall. The gateway tower on the opposite front was extended by a barbican; and on either side of its inner portal two broad straight stairs led up to the first floor rooms and finally to the curtain wall-walks.

For its period, the two-storeyed suite of buildings round the curtain is exceptionally well designed. Proceeding counter-clockwise from the gate, we have in succession the kitchen, at ground level but rising through the full height of the buildings: a service passage, with a hatch from the kitchen at ground level, and no doubt a wooden stair ascending to the hall; the great hall, solar (or retiring room) and *camera* (or private room)—all following on in normal succession and (save the kitchen) raised over cellarage. These living rooms open one from another in the usual way. Between the solar and *camera* is a small ante-room, with a wide opening from the *camera* into the chapel, so that the lord could take part in the services conducted by his chaplain. On such occasions, as often in medieval houses, the ante-room would in effect become a nave, the chapel proper serving as the chancel.

So far all is straightforward, in the normal sequence of a large medieval house. But at the far end of the *camera* we encounter a blind wall, beyond which is a *second hall*, entered from the opposite end, by the stair leading up from the courtyard. According to Dr Ralegh Radford, this second hall was the guest chamber. But it is noteworthy that whereas all the other living quarters, except the small ante-room, have ample fireplaces, the so-called guest chamber has none. If heated at all, it must have been by a central hearth, with a louvre. Again, while all the other living rooms have ample windows pierced through the old curtain wall, as well as on the courtyard front, the so-called guest chamber has none on the outside. It is not to be thought that the Earl of Cornwall desired to provide his guests with accommodation less comfortable than that of his own *familia*. Surely, therefore, the late Mr Sidney Toy was right in recognising this second hall as the 'hall of the guard'. It is in fact a mess-hall or barrack room, providing for a small standing garrison of men-at-arms. It is therefore an early and important example of the changes wrought upon the castle plan by the development of 'bastard feudalism', to be discussed in Chapter 10. The position of this barrack-hall at Restormel, on the left side of the main entrance, recalls that of the barrack-hall at Llawhaden Castle in Pembrokeshire. It also closely resembles the barrack-hall at the Scottish castle of Dunnottar, which likewise has no fireplace. A point to note about the Restormel barrack is that, while the other roofs are flat, the barrack room had a loft between gables, evidently to serve as sleeping quarters for the men.

In the courtyard a deep pit gives access to the well, with a total depth of 50 feet.

The basement under the barrack-hall has two doors. Here therefore will have been the stable for six horses, mentioned in a survey of 1337, which has thus been anglicized by Mr Toy:

> There is a certain castle well-walled, and there are within the walls of the same castle one hall, three chambers and as many cellars, one chapel whereof the glass of the greater window is for a great part broken and needs speedy reparation lest it become worse, one image of Mary, of precious stone so it is said, in the same chapel in alabaster[1], two bells in the same, one weighing 100 lbs, which belonged to the hermitage lately of Friar Robert. One stable for six horses. Three chambers over the gate, covered with lead in a decayed state, and the leaves of the gate of the same castle are weak and insufficient.

The survey next proceeds to notice buildings outside the castle:

> And there are outside the gate of the said castle one great hall with two cellars and one convenient chapel; the kitchen of the same hall and a certain passage leading from the hall to the kitchen are ruinous and in need of speedy reparation. There are three chambers and three cellars below and one bakehouse out of repair, and two stables for twenty horses on either side of the gate, these old and ruinous, and there is there a certain water conduit made of lead through which water is conveyed into the castle to every domestic office therein, which wants to be newly repaired with lead.

There can be no possibility that these buildings 'outside the gate of the castle' were in a regular bailey. A Norman mound and court castle was a unit, and in such a survey the accommodation in both departments included together. Moreover, at Restormel such a bailey would be enclosed with massive earthworks on a scale matching the mount; while the bailey ditch would of course merge into the ditch enclosing the mount. When stone curtains were built around the bailey, these were invariably continued as 'wing-walls 'climbing up the *motte* to join the shell-keep on top. Of all this there is no trace at Restormel.

---

[1] These two words are a later insertion above the line, by someone who knew the material of the image.

The outbuildings on record will have been just such as one would expect: requisite to house the numerous visitors and their retinues coming and going at an important royal castle. A basecourt it may properly be called, and indeed is so termed by Leland in 1538; but certainly not the entrenched bailey of a first-class Norman castle, organic-ally bound up into its *motte*. Already about 1600 the basecourt is des-cribed as 'rather to be conjectured than discerned'. Today little remains but some traces of a bank and stone foundations.

The earliest recorded owners of Restormel bore the name of Fitz-Turstin; later owners that of Cardinham. By 1264 the latter had been succeeded by a family called Tracy. In the Barons' War the castle was held on behalf of Simon de Montfort: but after his death it passed to Richard, Earl of Cornwall and King of the Romans, brother of Henry III. Its subsequent history is bound up with that of the Earldom and later Duchy of Cornwall: today it is therefore an appanage of H.R.H. The Prince of Wales. As Duke of Cornwall, the Black Prince kept court twice at Restormel, in 1354 and again at Christmastide, 1362. Thereafter the castle seems to have been allowed to decay. In 1644, during the Cornish campaign, it was held against the King, but sur-rendered to Sir Richard Grenville after a brief resistance. Though it does not then seem to have been 'slighted', after the final triumph of the Roundheads a Parliamentary Commission reported in 1649 that the 'said castle is utterly ruined, nothing but the out walls thereof remaining, which are not where they stand worth the taking down'. In 1925 the Commissioners of the Duchy of Cornwall handed over the castle to the guardianship of the then Office of Works.

4

Stone Keeps of Norman and Angevin Times

In the last chapter we have considered a selection of the formidable earthwork castles which the Normans threw up to guard the land of which William the Conqueror and his followers had taken seisin on the stricken field of Hastings, and in the cruel campaigns in the north that followed.

> Cold heart and bloody hand
> Now rule English land

lamented a Norse poet of the time. What may be termed the conventional view of the Norman Conquest was stated by a well-known historian in the early years of this century. In the national character of the later Saxons, he is prepared to concede:

> There was still much good metal, but if the Anglo-Saxon was to do anything worth doing in the world, it was necessary that it should be passed through the fire and hammered on the anvil. The fire and the anvil were about to be supplied with unsparing hand by the Norman conquerors.

This may sound in the ears of some folk rather too much like the arguments one heard on behalf of the *Herrenvolk* in Hitler's Germany. Other students of the Norman Conquest are not quite so sure. I have already described its consequences as a cultural catastrophe. This opinion can be buttressed by much evidence other than that furnished by coinage and manuscript illumination and architecture. On far wider grounds, it can be claimed that the Norman Conquest, by embroiling England in continental affairs, distorted her development. In particular, it involved her in the grotesque Plantagenet empire of Henry II, a historical absurdity which ran counter to the whole national-istic trend of the later Middle Ages, and resulted finally in the political and social catastrophe, alike for England and France, of the Hundred Years' War. The effect of this European involvement was to direct England from what should have been her historical role, to achieve the unity of Great Britain. The statesmanlike policy of Edward I to bring this about by a marriage of his son with the heiress of the Scottish throne was foiled by the hand of fate; and the English king's misguided attempt to bring it about by force led to three centuries of bitter and ruinous war between two countries which surely should have been natural partners. The effect of all this upon the subject of our special study, the development of the English castle, will become fully apparent in subsequent chapters of this book.

For the present, our concern is with Norman castles. When we admire them today, when we acknowledge that their subsequent history associates many of them with our proudest national memories, let us never forget the bitter oppression of which in their origin they were the symbol in England's green and pleasant land.

Right from the outset of the Conquest, these prideful earthworks were accompanied, in some few cases, by the alternative theme of the massive four-square stone tower—the 'Norman keep' of historical romances and popular imagination. By far the most famous of these is the mighty donjon which the Conqueror built to overawe the citizens of his capital, and which ever since has given its name to the vast com-plex castle of many dates that we still call the Tower of London.[1] Another of the Conqueror's stone keeps, in some respects the most remarkable of all its class, is COLCHESTER CASTLE in Essex. As everyone knows, Colchester is the *Camulodunum* of the Romans, and before them the royal capital of Cunobelin, King of the Trinovantes, the Cymbeline of Shakespeare. His coins, minted at Camulodunum, display his name in fair Latin letters, and on the reverse the town's name and a head of

---

[1] For a brief account and analysis of the Tower, reference may be permitted to Chapter IX of my *Exploring Castles*.

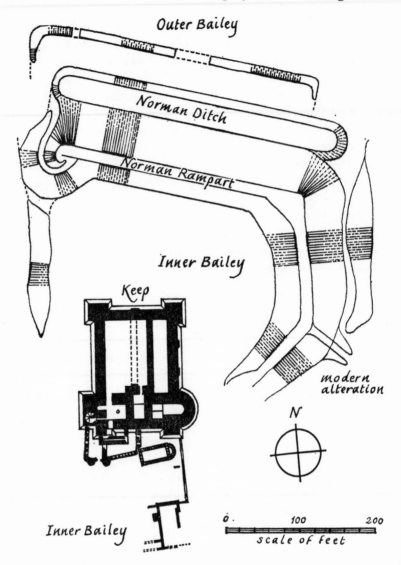

Plan of Colchester Castle

wheat, doubtless in salute to the agricultural prosperity of his reign. The Romans made Camulodunum the seat of their first British *colonia*, or settlement of time-expired veterans—building, as was their wont, their new city on a site somewhat apart from that of the Celtic *oppidum*.

The principal public building of the Roman city was the temple of Claudius, erected in honour of the Emperor under whom the Roman conquest was begun. In the vivid narrative of Tacitus we are told how in A.D. 60 Camulodunum was given to the flames during the insurrection of Boudicea. He tells us about the portents that affrighted the inhabitants of the colony before the storm broke. The statue of Victory in the temple fell down; hollow cries in an unknown tongue were heard in the Town House, and wailings in the theatre; in the streets frenzied women proclaimed that destruction was at hand. And so in due course it came to pass. The town was stormed, sacked and burnt. The survivors fled into the temple; but within a couple of days this also was carried by assault, and served with the like fate. It is one of the most dramatic things in British archaeology that the massive foundations of this Temple of Claudius, still bearing marks of the conflagration, survive beneath the Conqueror's castle, which is exactly positioned by the temple, and which itself is largely built out of Roman materials. Clearly the stance and dimensions of William the Conqueror's castle have been fixed by the Roman temple dedicated, a thousand years before, to a predecessor in the invasion of Britain, Tiberius Claudius Caesar Augustus. The Roman temple stood within a large handsome colonnaded courtyard, considerable remains of which have been revealed by excavation.

With over-all dimensions of $151\frac{1}{2}$ feet by 110 feet, Colchester is the largest of all our Norman keeps—not only in Britain, but anywhere in Europe. This astounding tower is now only two storeys in height. Formerly it had a third; but even in its complete condition, horizontal spread rather than brow-beating altitude must have been the keynote of the theme. Reduced in height though it is, the keep has obviously been erected in two 'builds', though doubtless with no great interval between them: for on the east front in particular, but also elsewhere round the building, a row of battlements may be discerned, with broad merlons and narrow embrasures—all sealed up beneath the later heightening, like fossils in a geological stratum. Three corners of this astounding structure are capped by broad, boldly projected towers: the south-east corner is set forward to house the semicircular apse of the chapel—in just the same way as in the much smaller Tower of London. In characteristic Norman fashion, the broad wall-faces of the keep are strengthened by flat pilaster-buttresses. As might be expected, Colchester

Castle is largely built out of Roman materials. What is interesting is that not only Roman stones and bricks have been used, but also the Roman manner of building, regular courses of stone work being separated by bonding courses of brick or tile. All these materials were ready to hand in the wreck of Camulodunum. But for some of the dressed work, stone was brought in from Barnack in Northamptonshire, and even imported from Caen in Normandy. Internally, much use was made of the characteristic early Norman technique of herring-bone work.

The entrance doorway at the west end of the south front was re-fashioned early in the twelfth century. It is a noble specimen of advanced Romanesque work. Within it, to the left, in the south-west tower, is the largest and finest of all our Norman spiral stairs, circling up clockwise to the summit of the keep. By this leftward turn of the stair, a result is achieved well understood by our castle builders: the assailant fighting his way up found his sword arm hemmed by the newel or stair-post, while the defender above him had the well of the stair free for his right hand to strike down at the aggressor. In the east shoulder of the north-west angle tower, at first floor level, is a postern door, which was reached by a stair ascending along the adjoining main wall-face. From this level upwards the corner tower contains a spiral stair.

The spacious interior of the tower was divided into three compartments by two longitudinal walls, placed surprisingly close to each other; but little can now be made out of the former internal arrangements. The fireplaces, original Norman work, are curious: their flues are not carried up into chimneys, but slope backwards so as to vent by double openings in the outer wall. They must have smoked abominably! The keep is well furnished with privies; and in its basement is a deep well. Long a bare empty shell, this grandest of all our Norman keeps has been fitted up as an antiquarian museum, displaying the whole history of Colchester from Belgic to modern times. This adaptation of a gutted Norman keep for modern cultural purposes has been achieved with consummate skill, in such a way as to need the minimum interference with the display of the precious contents, while at the same time hiding as little as possible the medieval walls.

No visitor to Colchester Castle should omit to look at the quaint carvings and graffiti with which former sojourners within the keep—whether voluntary or by compulsion—have occupied their idle moments in inscribing upon its walls. These included spirited portraits of thirteenth-century horse and foot soldiers; a figure of St Christopher of carrying the Infant Christ; and the names of a fourteenth-century jailer and his wife.

Of course this colossal keep did not stand naked before its assailants. Towards the north and east lie massive remains of banks and ditches, defences of the Norman bailey. Within this enclosure, a simple obelisk commemorates the heroic defenders of Colchester, Sir Charles Lucas and Sir George Lisle, who held the town for twelve weeks on behalf of Charles I, and on its honourable surrender were shot in cold blood within the castle garth by the godly Puritans (28 August 1648). One does not require to be a Cavalier without subscribing, in substance if not perhaps in language, to the robust verdict of a contemporary Royalist historian, who comments upon 'this odious fact, for which the sufferers' memories, and the due renown of their virtue and valour shall flourish, and the names of those bloodthirsty men that perpetrated and counselled it, shall stink and rot'. All history, from the Old Testament onwards, teaches us that the cruellest form of government so far devised by man is a militant theocracy.

It is obvious that the Tower of London and the far greater keep at Colchester were designed by the same architect. But whereas the Tower was intended to keep in order the turbulent citizens of the capital, Colchester keep was almost certainly built to guard against the expected Danish invasion of 1083. Hence the signs of haste in its workmanship, in particular the temporary finishing-off of the walls with a defensive parapet before the tower had been carried up to its full height. The invasion did not come off, so the building was completed at leisure; and the last stage obviously was the substitution of the original pro-visional entrance by a more dignified portal in the rich Norman style, worthy of a first-class royal castle. In the thirteenth century the entrance to the keep was strengthened by a barbican, and stone walls and towers partly replaced the earthworks of the bailey. The history of Colchester Castle has been comparatively uneventful, though it has a sad record as a jail—the most poignant case being undoubtedly that of the Quaker lad James Parnell, who in 1655 died of cold and hunger and maltreat-ment in the tower prison. He is our first British Quaker martyr. His monument inside the castle, and that of the two Royalist leaders in the castle grounds, commemorating victims from opposite ends of the politico-religious spectrum, form a unique and scorching indictment of Puritan fanaticism under the Cromwellian regime.

One of the most remarkable things to be seen at Colchester Castle is the remains of an early chapel, with a semi-circular apse, in the ditch in the front of the tower. This chapel has been faced inside and outside with marble, and in view of this and its abnormal position with reference to the medieval tower, it is difficult to resist the conclusion that here we have the Christian church of Roman or sub-Roman Camulodunum. Further out, some remains, not now exposed, have been found of the medieval great hall. Here, therefore, at Colchester Castle we have an archaeological complex hardly paralleled in Britain. No wonder that a visiting German antiquary recently expressed his utter astonishment that the whole area had not long since been thoroughly investigated and every surviving foundation laid bare.

At Colchester, then, the fair county of Essex provides us with our largest Norman stone keep. In HEDINGHAM CASTLE the same county can boast the most beautiful among them all. Tall, superbly proportioned, and faced with the finest ashlar masonry, this noble keep of the de Veres, Earls of Oxford, stands within the vast earthworks of a *motte* and bailey. The *motte* has a summit area of about two acres. Evidently it is natural in substance, otherwise it could scarcely have carried the ponderous weight of the great stone tower. To the east lies the bailey, now occupied by a fine Queen Anne mansion. On the *motte* were formerly besides the keep, a hall, chapel and other buildings: in view of this, and of the comparative insignificance of the bailey, it seems that we have here not so much a *motte* as a ring castle, like Restormel. Bailey and *motte* are now united by a brick Tudor bridge, with four pointed arches. Few will dispute the claim of the great tower of Hedingham Castle to be 'the most striking and the best preserved of the tall Norman keeps'. For its superb effect it relies, not only on its splendid masonry of Barnack Oolite, but on the grand simplicity of its architecture. The four-storeyed tower rests upon a boldly outspread plinth: at two of its four corners rectangular turrets rise 20 feet above the wall heads, to which they give access; the main wall faces carry the usual flat pilasters; the windows, paired at the level of the internal gallery, are of simple Norman character—though the upper ones are shafted and moulded

8   *The Barbican, Lewes Castle*

with the chevron pattern. The handsome, triply chevron-moulded Norman door, which is on the first floor, was reached by a forework, of

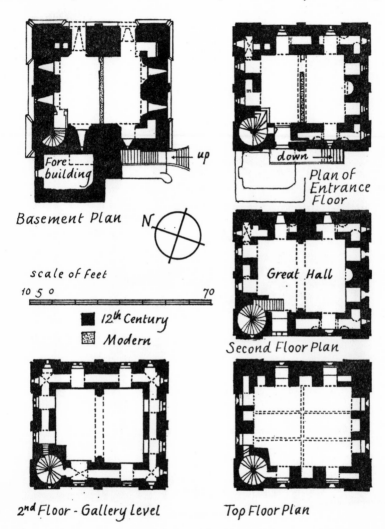

Fore building

Basement Plan

N

scale of feet
10 5 0   70

■ 12th Century
▨ Modern

up

down

Plan of Entrance Floor

Great Hall

Second Floor Plan

2nd Floor - Gallery level

Top Floor Plan

Plan of Hedingham Keep

which little but the stair and the roof-raggle now remains. Evidently this forework was an afterthought. The doorway was defended by a portcullis. Somewhat remarkable for so large a keep—the over-all

9   *The Keep, Hedingham Castle*

dimensions, above the basal apron, are about 62 feet by 55 feet—the interiors have not been vaulted; but the timbers of the two main floors

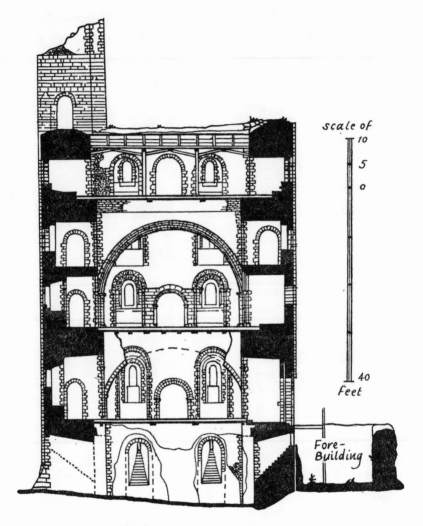

Hedingham Castle—Section through Keep

are carried on splendid flying arches, each of about 28 feet in span. Each arch is of two orders, resting upon wall shafts and cushion caps. Above ground level the walls are honeycombed with closets; while in the upper portion of the great hall the entire circuit of the tower is traversed by a mural passage, like the triforium gallery of a church, passing though all the window bays, and communicating with the single spiral stair in the north-west turret, which serves the whole building from the basement to the flat leaded roof. To the top of the stair turret the external height is over 100 feet. Like almost all Norman keeps, this one contains a well, which is placed in the north-eastern turret. Although the fireplaces and the rear arches of the windows are shafted and decorated with chevron pattern, internally as on the outside, this noble tower maintains an aspect of virginal austerity. The fireplaces vent through the outer wall in the same way as in Colchester. Strangely enough for so distinguished a building, it possesses inside the tower neither kitchen nor chapel. There is no record of its erection, but it may be dated with confidence, upon grounds of style, to the period of Henry I. An interesting feature of this splendid tower is that the putlog holes used in its construction have been left open, so that fresh scaffolding could be inserted when the external masonry required re-pointing or repair.

Throughout its active history Hedingham Castle remained almost continuously a principal seat of the puissant house of Oxford, and the rich tomb of the fifteenth Earl and his Countess may still be seen in the adjoining parish church of Castle Hedingham. In Chapter 10 we shall have something to say about 'bastard feudalism', under which great magnates kept armed retainers to enforce their will, particularly during the anarchic days of the Wars of the Roses. This vicious practice was finally stamped out by Henry VII, who passed stringent laws against the maintaining of such armed retainers. In his famous *Historie of the Raigne of King Henry the Seventh*, Bacon tells us a remarkable story of a visit paid by the King to the Earl of Oxford at Hedingham Castle:

At the King's going away, the Earl's servants stood (in a seemly manner) in their livery coats, with cognisances, ranged on both sides, and made the King a lane. The King called the Earl to him, and said 'My Lord, I have heard much of your hospitality, but I see it is greater than the speech. These handsome gentlemen and yeomen, which I see on both sides of me, are sure your menial servants.' The Earl smiled, and said, 'It may please your Grace, that were not for mine ease. They are most of them my retainers, that are come to do me service at such a time as this, and chiefly to see your Grace.' The King started a little and said 'By my faith (my lord) I thank you for my good cheer, but I may not endure to have my laws broken in my sight. My attorney must speak with you.' And it is part of the report that the Earl compounded for no less than fifteen thousand marks.

In more modern times Hedingham Castle has been well maintained by its owners. But at some time two doors had been broken into the basement of the tower, which was used as a wood store for the adjoining mansion. On 23 September 1918, the keep was gutted by a fire. The blaze spread with rapidity upwards and downwards, until the wood-stack in the basement was consumed. So great was the forced draught that the burning tower resembled an active volcano. Everything was over before the fire engines arrived, so that no water was played upon the keep. This saved the tower from splitting asunder, or at least from irreparable damage to its superb ashlar masonry. As it was, the tower cooled gradually; and except for quite minor flaking of the stonework the only visible effect is that, while the exterior masonry is grey in colour, the interior is now a warm pink. The tower was thereafter restored by the Ancient Monuments branch of the then Office of Works. In the triforium gallery are many inscriptions, some as old as the seventeenth century. There is also an exceptionally fine suite of large mason's marks.

Another great Norman keep, distinguished by its excellent masonry and refined architectural detail, is to be found in the castle which from its lofty crag so proudly dominates the pleasant Yorkshire resort of SCARBOROUGH. Here we encounter an archaeological complex stretching even further into the 'dark backward and abyss of time' than we found at Colchester.

Probably about seven centuries before the birth of Christ, a small community of refugees from the Continent, driven westward, as we may guess, by other races pressing them from behind, took to their boats. Safely crossing the tumbling waters of the North Sea, they landed beneath the mighty promontory of Scarborough. Hereabouts they settled; but what was to become the Castle Hill they occupied only during the summer season—no doubt seeking more sheltered quarters when the bitter gales blew in across the waste of wintry waters. The refuse pits which they dug tell us much about their mode of life. They possessed herds of oxen and flocks of sheep, with dogs to guard them; they also had tame horses, whose flesh they sometimes ate. Whether they cultivated cereals is not so certain; and there is no evidence that they availed themselves of the food resources of the sea. For cooking they used earthen pots. These they sunk in pits and partly filled with water, which they brought to the boil by dropping in red-hot pebbles. The women wove clothes, the menfolk made themselves tools and weapons of stone and bronze, and had even some acquaintance with iron. Personal ornaments were made of Whitby jet, glass and Baltic amber.

What became of these primitive refugees we know not. A thousand years later their summer squatting ground was occupied by Imperial Rome, in what was to prove a last effort to keep the English out of Britain. In the year A.D. 367 the defences of Roman Britain suddenly collapsed, like a pack of stacked cards, before a triple assault from the Picts beyond Hadrian's Wall, the Scots crossing over from Ireland, and the Saxons faring west-overseas. But the work of Rome in Britain was not yet done. The situation was restored by a great general, Count Theodosius, father of the famous Emperor of the same name. Hadrian's Wall and its supporting stations were repaired and garrisoned anew. To protect the rearward flank of the restored frontier against the Saxon raiders, a new system of coastal defence in depth was devised, with Roman thoroughness and skill. The front line of this organisation was provided by a chain of fortified signal stations along the Yorkshire coast. One of these coastguard posts was placed upon the Castle Hill of Scarborough—right on top of the prehistoric settlement. Like all the others, it consisted of a substantial four-square tower of stone, carried up doubtless to a considerable height, from which smoke signals and semaphore messages could be sent by day, and fire signals at night. Round the base of the tower was a square walled enclosure with round angle-bastions, so as to provide shelter for the watch, and perhaps their steeds and stores. Outside all was a broad and deep ditch. Excavation of these Yorkshire coastguard stations has shown that they continued to be manned until the opening years of the fifth century, when they perished by violence in the general collapse of the Roman defences in the North. The Scarborough station was burnt. In others have been found the hacked and slashed skeletons of their slaughtered defenders and their wives and bairns, huddled together, or in one case pitched into

a well, after they had fallen in the final assault. It is impossible, therefore, to look upon the excavated remains of our Scarborough signal
station without emotion. Here we stand before the grave of an empire
—the Roman Empire, the greatest, and (with all its faults) the most
successful and beneficent political achievement of the human race of
which history bears record.

Where Rome had failed with the sword she returned to conquer by
the Cross. Some centuries after the establishment of the Anglian kingdom of Deira, a small early Christian chapel was built within the
foundations of the Roman coastguard tower. After the founding of the
Norman keep this early oratory was rebuilt in an ornate style; and in the
later Middle Ages this was progressively extended as the private chapel
of the castle, a small vestry being added for the chaplain. The little
establishment was provided with its own wall. Since the chapel was
surrounded by a cemetery, this burial ground must be anterior to that
of the twelfth-century parish church of St Mary, down below in the
borough. The little chapel may therefore justly be venerated as the
matrix ecclesia of Scarborough.

The great Norman keep was erected by Henry II between 1158 and
1175. Unfortunately little more than half of this noble tower remains,
the rest having been demolished during the Civil War. Externally it
measures about 55 feet square, and it must have been about 100 feet in
height. Like Hedingham Castle, it comprises four unvaulted storeys, and
the main floor was spanned by a noble flying arch. On the south side
there was a forework, containing a stair of access to the main door on
the first floor. The tower is faced with fine dark red sandstone ashlar,
and the architectural details, though plain, are excellent, alike in design
and execution. Its roof was leaded. The whole area of the headland,
amounting to no less than 19 acres, and rising sheer about 250 feet above
the sea, was included in the castle, and is protected against the town by
a long curtain wall, over 20 feet high, with a wide ditch outside. This
wall seems mostly of Norman date, but half-round towers were added in
the thirteenth century. Anticipating a practice later common (see p.
105), the keep is placed in the fore-front of the enclosure, to command
the entrance, which is further secured by a long and elaborately fortified
thirteenth-century barbican, straddling the ditch. The area round the
keep is walled and ditched so as to provide what was called the 'inner
ward'. It contains a well, about 170 feet deep—the upper 68 feet faced

with stone, the remainder quarried in the live rock. This inner ward forms little more than a curtilage to the keep; the hall, kitchen and other domestic buildings were outside, in the main enclosure or 'castle garth'. In 1538 the 'sea-cliff' is described as 'without wall, tower or turret'; but it was noted that there were 'three places in the same that men may climb up'.

In the medieval history of Scarborough Castle the most famous event was its defence against the irate barons in 1312 by Edward II's favourite, Piers Gaveston, Earl of Cornwall, who was forced by starvation to surrender, and thereafter was murdered under trust. This black deed, which forms the turning point of Marlowe's tragedy, deprived the baronial opposition to Edward II's misgovernment of every shred of moral authority, and prepared the way for the king's final triumph and revenge at Boroughbridge ten years later.

Twice strenuously besieged by the Roundheads in the Civil War, on its second capture the castle was dismantled, the keep being partly blown up by a mine. This, however, was by no means the end of the military history of the castle. After the Forty-five, barracks, using the foundations of an ancient building, were built within the main courtyard; and in the later nineteenth century a coastguard station was erected—though the builders knew it not—right on top of its Roman predecessor! On 16 December 1914, a German squadron bombarded the town, firing about 500 shells. Much destruction was caused in the castle, the barracks and coastguard station were wrecked, and the keep sustained minor damage.

The masonry of Colchester is peculiar to itself, owing to the re-use of Roman materials. The keeps of Hedingham and Scarborough are faced with fine ashlar. The keep of ROCHESTER is built of rough coursed rubble, which in the thirteenth century was lime-washed—as was also the Tower of London, hence its *soubriquet* of the 'White Tower'. Rochester was the Roman *Durobrivae*, a small town. Its walls were patched up by Saxon kings, and just outside them William the Conqueror threw up a *motte*, the remains of which are today known as Boley Hill. Presumably this name is a corruption of 'bailey'. The lofty keep, 'a masterpiece of Norman architecture', is accurately documented to 1126-39. Excluding the fore-building, it measures 70 feet square,

and rises 125 feet to the battlements of its four corner turrets, being
thus the tallest of our Norman keeps. Both on these turrets and on the
tower itself the battlements are well preserved, while the main structure
displays in addition the putlog holes for a bretasche or timber war-head.
The keep is unvaulted, and through all its four storeys it is divided by a
cross-wall; on the main floor this becomes a noble Norman arcade, the
piers of which are built of fine ashlar. From basement to garret, this cross-
wall is pierced by the well-shaft, which traverses the central pier of the
arcade. As at Hedingham, the upper level of the hall is traversed by a
mural gallery, passing through all the numerous window bays, and
connecting the two spiral stairs, which are placed in diagonally opposite
turrets, north-east and south-west. Of these, the former stair rises
through the whole height of the keep, while the latter starts from the
first floor. It is difficult to surmise what purpose these galleries were
meant to serve, unless to permit access to the upper windows, when
these required attention. But when Henry III stayed in the castle he
seems to have occupied the hall, and complained of the disturbance
caused by members of the garrison on their way to the chapel. Since
it can hardly be imagined that they would have invaded the royal
privacy by actually passing through the room where the King was
lodged, we may infer that the soldiery occupied the top storey of the
tower—convenient at need to man the battlements—and that they made
their way down to the chapel *via* the south-west stair and along the
mural gallery.

Each division of the tower was covered by a low pitched roof, with a
central 'valley' resting on the cross-wall, and providing for drainage.
The keep is well furnished with windows large or small, fireplaces
venting outward through the wall, privies and wall-presses. At the
south-east corner the original square turret has been replaced by a
round angle tower; the reason for this we shall discover in the next
paragraph. An interesting feature at Rochester Castle is the well-
preserved forework. This begins as an open stair rising along the west
face of the north-west turret, turning the corner and continuing through
a handsome Norman doorway, defended by a portcullis. Below the
vestibule are two vaulted prisons; above it is the castle chapel, in a
plain but good Norman style. It comprises nave and chancel, the latter
vaulted.

The most famous incident in the history of Rochester Castle was its

10 Scarborough Castle

three months' siege by King John in 1216. His military engines having failed to batter down the walls, the King had recourse to mining, by which means he first brought down the curtain wall, and then the south-west angle of the keep. In the succeeding reign both were repaired, the curtain with a round tower and the keep with the round angle turret mentioned above, which is solid save for two loopholes at first floor level.

During the siege William de Albini (Daubeny), who held the castle for the insurgent barons, noted an archer of his garrison taking deliberate aim at King John with his crossbow. The governor at once struck up the archer's weapon, forbidding him to slay the Lord's Anointed. In the language of *1066 and All That*, this was a *Bad Thing*.

In the Barons' War of 1264 Rochester Castle was held for the King by Earl Warrenne, and underwent a second siege at the hands of Simon de Montfort. Once again the outer curtain was sapped, but the keep held out until rescued by a royalist force coming from Nottingham. The relieving troops covered the 160 miles in a remarkable forced march of five days. During the Peasants' Revolt in 1381, in which the men of Kent, always notorious for their turbulence, bore a leading part, the castle fell to the insurgents.

Even in the strict selection imposed by the scale of this work, space must be found for some account of the mighty Northumbrian rock-perched castle of BAMBURGH—if only for the unique part it has played in our history since the first landing here of the Angles in 547. Upon this darkly beetling crag, Ida, founder of the Anglian kingdom of Bernicia, built 'timbered Bebbanburh, that was first with hedge surrounded and thereafter with wall'. As a modern historian has justly observed,

> it was the ascendancy of the English kings whose throne was firmly established on the basaltic ramparts of Bamburgh during the most crucial period of our national history, that gave the English name to the land that was already being called a New Saxony, and the final unification of which was destined to be achieved by Saxon sovereigns.

By the Celts whom the Angles displaced the rock was known as Din Guarydi: and it is a Celtic scribe who tells us how Ethelfrith, grandson of Ida,

11 The Keep, Rochester Castle

gave Din Guarydi to his wife. She was called Bebbab; and from the name of his wife the place received its name of Bebbanburh.

After the great battle of Heavenfield (674), which finally secured the triumph of Christianity in Northumbria, the saintly King Oswald united the two kingdoms of Bernicia and Deira, that is to say, all England north of the Humber. In the eloquent language of another modern historian:

> Thus, then did Bamburgh, which is now a lonely village by the German Ocean, become 'the royal city', the most strongly fortified abode of the most powerful king in Britain, the centre of a realm which stretched from the Humber to the Firth of Forth, and apparently, through the rest of the seventh century, the destined capital of England, if England should ever attain unity. The traveller who now visits this dethroned queen of Northumbria will see much that, however noble and picturesque, must be eliminated by an effort of the imagination if he would picture to himself the Bamburgh of King Oswald. The massive keep that 'stands foursquare to every wind that blows' dates from the reign of Henry II; the great hall of the castle, now ingeniously restored by a modern architect, was originally of the time of Edward I; some of the still existing buildings were reared by a benevolent ecclesiastic in the reign of George III; but the natural features of the place are unchangeable and unchanged, and in looking upon them we know that we behold the same scenes that met the eye of the conqueror of Cadwallon. Such is the rock itself, an upheaved mass of basalt upon whose black sides the tooth of time seems to gnaw in vain; such are the long sandy dunes which gather around its base; such the Inner and Outer Farne Islands, fragments of basalt rising out of the ocean at distances ranging from three to six miles from the castle; such the far-off peninsula, which when the tide flows becomes Holy Island; such the long range of Cheviot on the western horizon, snow-covered for many months of the year. Such, we might almost say, is the fierce wind which, from one quarter or another, seems for ever attacking the lonely fortress, and which assuredly battered the 'timbered' palace of Oswald as it now batters the time-worn fortress of the Plantangenet.

It lies outwith the scope of this book to present, even in outline, the stormy and colourful history of Bamburgh in Anglo-Saxon times. Our concern is with the medieval castle. The Norman Conquest found the place long divested of any political significance and reduced indeed, to a low estate. 'She who was once the mistress of the cities of Britain' laments a chronicler, 'has now been brought down to the condition of a handmaiden'. Yet the keen military eye of the Conqueror could not overlook the strategic and tactical importance of the site, so near the frontier of a Scotland now ruled by the powerful and aggressive Malcolm Canmore. So before the end of William's reign the rock of Bamburgh emerges as a strong castle. Some of the tenants of the royal *vil* held their lands by the curious service of carting logs for the king's hearth in the castle. During the rebellion of 1095 Robert de Mowbray, Earl of Northumberland, held Bamburgh against William II, who besieged the castle in person, erecting over against it a *malvoisin* or wooden counter-fort, like that whose earthworks are still to be seen below Corfe Castle—doubtless a relic of the siege by King Stephen in 1139. The Earl escaped, but the castle continued to hold out under his gallant young Countess, until the Red King, having captured her husband, paraded him before the castle, after sending in a message that unless she submitted his eyes would be torn out!

The great tower of the castle was in course of erection between 1164 and 1170. Much building went on during the reign of John and Henry III. In the first War of Scottish Independence Bamburgh appears to have played no very active part. On the contrary, it was neglected, and at the accession of Edward III (1327) the buildings were found to be in a shocking state. Nevertheless by the outbreak of the Second War the castle had been repaired and provisioned so that in 1333 it could offer a successful resistance to a formidable attack by the Scots. To Bamburgh in 1346 was brought the captive King David II of Scotland, sorely wounded at Neville's Cross. Surgeons were called in from York to extract the arrow which had lodged deeply in his body; their expenses and fee amounted to £6. Presumably 'Davy's Tower', on the south-west curtain, was where the wounded king was tended. A lurid glimpse into the insanitary customs of the Middle Ages—though surely this particular case will have been exceptional—is the report of a commission of inquiry into the state of the castle in 1372, which among other irregularities informs us that the water supply of the keep here was unusable because the well had become choked with the guts of slaughtered cattle! We are not surprised to learn that the rope and bucket had been stolen.

It was during the Wars of the Roses that Bamburgh Castle played its greatest part upon the stage of English medieval history. Its two sieges by the Yorkists, in 1462 and 1464, in which heavy cannon were employed, both resulted in the unconditional surrender of the fortress. Before the commencement of the second siege, a final summons to surrender declared the anxiety of King Edward IV to avoid the necessity of bombarding 'this jewel, the which our most dread sovereign lord hath so greatly in favour, seeing it marches so nigh his ancient enemies of Scotland, he specially desires to have it whole, unbroken with ordinance'. If therefore the obstinacy of the defenders should render a bombardment necessary, the grim warning followed, that for every shot fired against its walls one of the defenders should lose his head. Undeterred, the garrison held out until before the impact of the cannon balls 'the stones flew into the sea'.

Thus honourably, in the service of the Red Rose, closes the active history of Bamburgh Castle. Although the eighteenth and nineteenth century restorations have bereft the vast pile of much of its architectural interest, it remains a most imposing structure, dominated by Henry II's stalwart keep. The walls of enceinte with their round and square towers enclose an area of nearly five acres; the greatest length of the long narrow site being not far short of a quarter of a mile, while the rock rises to a full 150 feet above the foreshore. The keep exhibits the rare peculiarity, due no doubt to the security of its site, of having the main entrance at ground level. Next in interest to the keep comes the roofless Norman Chapel of St Oswald, with nave, chancel, and semi-circular apse. The domestic apartments are arranged along the south side of the eastern or inner bailey. Except for some fine ribbed vaulting in the basement, these rooms are mostly modern.

The three most elaborately decorated Norman rectangular keeps in England are undoubtedly Castle Rising in Norfolk, Newcastle-upon-Tyne, and Norwich. The first two I have described elsewhere.[1] The keep of Newcastle is known to have been designed by the architect, Maurice the Engineer, who subsequently was responsible for the mightier keep at Dover; and indeed the resemblances in plan between these two towers are patent. The great tower at Norwich is distinguished

[1] Castle Rising, in *Castles in Britain*, pp. 15–18; Newcastle, in *Exploring Castles*, pp. 28–41.

beyond all others by its tiers of external arcading: but most of this face-work has been replaced in modern times, while the internal features have been almost obliterated by the use of the tower first as a prison and latterly as a museum. The keep and its outbuildings stand on the truncated stump of a *motte* of unusual size. But it is impossible to pursue further the fascinating subject of our Norman square keeps, of which hundreds, great and small, still survive up and down the country. Rather it is time for us now to turn our attention to a major change in the design of the donjon tower which took place in England, as in France, during Angevin times—that is to say, from about the last quarter of the twelfth century.

This change consisted in building the donjon tower round instead of square. A round tower has three obvious advantages over a square one. In the first place, it presents no angles to an assailant; and an angle is always a weak point in a military structure. Here the battering ram or the miner's pick can be used to dislodge the corner-stones of the tower. Or, if a sap is being employed, the engineers will mine under the corner of the tower, so that its collapse will bring down a greater or lesser extent of the adjoining walls. This was the method employed by King John to break into Rochester keep. Secondly a round tower readily permits of being dome-vaulted on all or at least its principal floors, and thus rendered largely fireproof. And thirdly, volumetrically, area for area, a round tower is more economical of masonry than a square one: for its walls are of the same thickness all round, whereas in a rectangular tower a greater thickness of masonry is of course required at the four corners.

Possibly the earliest, and certainly the most remarkable examples of the new fashion of donjon are the great towers of CONISBROUGH in Yorkshire and ORFORD in Suffolk. It will be convenient to consider them together. The late Sir William St John Hope considered the Conis-brough donjon to be 'one of the finest pieces of twelfth-century masonry in existence', and has recorded his opinion of its date and builder thus: 'not improbably, from its likeness to the great tower of Orford Castle in Suffolk, which was in building from 1170 to 1175, and onwards, about 1170 by Hamelin, Earl of Surrey, the husband of the heiress of the Warrennes'. With the proposed dating none will disagree; but I consider the likeness of Orford to Conisbrough more apparent than real. Practically the only thing that they really share in common is that both are, in principle, circular donjons—although the external outline of Orford is in fact multangular. The six symmetrically disposed projections which break the cylindrical outline of Conisbrough are strictly buttresses. Their function is architectonic; and it is only incidentally that one of them is made use of to house the chapel. At

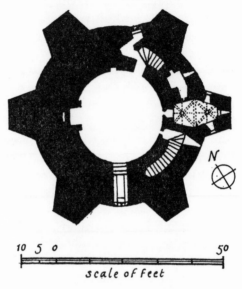

Plan of Conisbrough Keep. Third floor

Orford, by contrast, the three large rectangular projections are wings designed to supply additional accommodation—two kitchens, a chapel, and a number of ingeniously practised closets, opening off the large halls in the central structure. One of these wings, indeed, is a regularly designed forework, such as is commonly found in the rectangular Norman keeps. Conisbrough has no such feature, the entrance on the first floor being reached by an open stair, set at right angles to the tower. At Orford one spiral stair, ascending from base to summit, serves all the floors, and another spiral stair communicates between the lower hall and a mezzanine closet in one of the projections. This is a different scheme from what we find at Conisbrough, where there is but one system of stairs, curving round in the circular wall of the tower, and arranged in flights starting from opposite sides on each floor, so that anybody ascending the tower has to cross each floor in turn. Such an arrangement, of course, has much to commend it on security grounds. For the rest, Orford, like Conisbrough, provides in its main apartments the standard tower-house accommodation—cellarage in the basement, common hall, lord's hall, and a fighting deck above. As often in Norman keeps, the chapel is on the first floor of the forework. The latrine

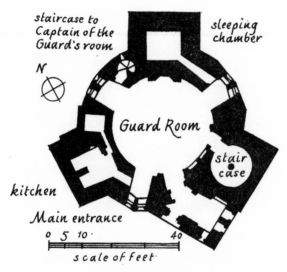

Plan of Orford Keep

accommodation at Orford is planned on a more lavish scale than at Conisbrough, and its domestic arrangements are more advanced. On the other hand the architectural detail appears to be earlier, or at least more archaic, than in the Yorkshire tower. Generally speaking, the Orford donjon looks more nearly akin to the rectangular Norman keeps, whereas Conisbrough seems to mark a new departure. The masonry of Conisbrough is superb ashlar, whereas that of Orford is well-coursed, squared flint rubble, with the numerous angles strongly emphasised in Caen stone.

The six great buttresses applied to the round tower of Conisbrough are remarkable. In the rectangular Norman keeps, the clasping buttresses at the four corners have their explanation both on general structural grounds, and also because they strengthen the angles, which (as we have noted above) are always the *point d'appui* favoured by the assailant with pick, battering ram, or the dreaded mine. But a round tower requires no such structural strengthening. Moreover, from a military standpoint the six buttresses are a positive drawback. They impede the command of the basal walls, both from the summit of the tower and from the adjoining curtains—all the more because the tower has not been provided for defence with a timber war-head.[1]

Both towers stand within mighty earthworks, which at Conisbrough, soon after the building of the donjon, were enclosed by a curtain wall. At Orford also there was an exterior towered curtain, but nothing of this now remains. As Orford was a royal castle, erected by Henry II between 1165 and 1173, its building records are fortunately preserved: the total cost was £1413 9s. 2d. Plainly it was built for coastal defence, but it has played little part in history. In the popular mind, the history of Conisbrough, as I pointed out at the beginning of this book, has been distorted through the fictitious glamour cast around it by the genius of Sir Walter Scott. The well-known story of how Earl Warrenne, in reply to Edward I's writ of *Quo Warranto* (1276), cast a rusty sword before the royal commissioners, with the proud defiance 'Here is my warrant: my ancestors won their lands with the sword, and with the sword will I keep them' may have been dramatised. But the official record bears witness that Warrenne could not, or would not, say on what terms he held the manor of Conisbrough, and that the royal commissioners were refused entrance to his castle, while his tenants were under strict orders to answer no questions. In the summer of 1317, during the private war between Earl Warrenne and Thomas, Earl of Lancaster, Conisbrough Castle fell into Lancaster's hands. This seems to have been the last occasion when it played a significant part in history. By the reign of Edward III it had become royal property; and 'nothing has generally proved more fatal to an independent historic estate than its absorption by the crown'.

Few grander spectacles exist in Britain than that provided by the mighty cylindrical donjon which towers above the proudly situated castle of PEMBROKE in South Wales. Its position, as an Anglo-Norman outpost

[1] For a discussion of Conisbrough Castle see my paper in *Archaeologia Aeliana*, 4th ser. vol. XXXIII, pp. 100–15.

in the far west of Celtic Wales, and the long succession of powerful and illustrious lords who from its walls have ruled broad territories in England, Wales, Ireland and Scotland, have ensured for this noble castle a memorable place in British history. Crowning a sheer lime-stone promontory washed by the tidal waters of Pembroke River and Monkton Pill, such a site must have attracted settlers from prehistoric times. Roman coins of Carausius and the House of Constantine seem to indicate the presence, in the first half of the fourth century, of a native community in trading relations with the more civilised areas of the Province. It was doubtless due to the phenomenal strength of its site that 'Pembroke owed its singular fortune among Welsh castles, in that it never fell, even temporarily, into the hands of the Welsh'. Space fails us to tell,even in outline, the story of the mighty barons who, from the time of its founder, Arnulph de Montgomery, in the reign of William II, have successively dwelt within and embellished this formid-able fortress. The Earldom of Pembroke dates from 1138, the first to hold the title being Gilbert de Clare, whose son, Richard Strongbow, is famous as the Anglo-Norman conqueror of Ireland. To the Clares succeeded the Marshals of England, taking their surname from this high office of state. Their effigies, skilfully pieced together after the havoc wrought by German bombs, still form one of the glories of the restored Temple Church in London. In turn the Marshals gave place to the great house of Valence, French kinsmen and favourites of Henry III. Among these the most celebrated was Aymer de Valence, Edward I's Viceroy of Scotland. After a distinguished career as soldier and states-man, he died in 1324, and lies in the noblest of all the great canopied altar-tombs in Westminster Abbey. Even the Scots, upon whom his hand was heavy, regarded him with respect. Barbour writes that Sir Aymer

was wise and wight,
And of his hand a worthy knight.

In 1456 the Countess of Richmond, widow of Jasper Tudor, gave birth at Pembroke Castle to a son who was to become Henry VII, the founder of the Tudor dynasty. After a stormy history during the great Civil War, the castle closed its active history in a long siege at the hands of Cromwell, whose heavy guns brought about the surrender of town and castle, after the heroic garrison had been reduced to a diet of

13 The Keep, Orford Castle

biscuits and rain-water. In the usual way the castle was thereafter dismantled. The outer curtain and its towers were part overthrown and part blown up. But the great donjon, no longer a serious military obstacle, was spared—doubtless on grounds of expense, for it was one of Cromwell's engaging habits to compel the inhabitants of towns which resisted him to pay for the cost of demolishing their own defences. At the same time the town walls were demolished, so that only fragments of them now remain.

Thus the proud donjon, which had survived the siege, escaped the final indignity of 'slighting'. We behold it now rising in undiminished majesty from its wide, apron-like plinth, to a height of 75 feet from ground level. Above the plinth the diameter is 53 feet. As it rises the wall gathers inwards with a gentle slope, and is further contracted by two offsets; so that (the interior face being vertical) just above the plinth the wall is about 15 feet thick, while at the top it is reduced in thickness by at least a foot. The masonry is roughly coursed grey limestone rubble, but buff-coloured sandstone is used for the sparse window openings—mere loopholes except in the two upper storeys, each of which has a double-lancet window. Of these the lower is enriched by a band of quatrefoil ornament, while the upper is plain. The tympanum above the lancets displays a corbel-head, of which the upper one leers down mockingly upon the spectator, 'possibly deriding those who should attack so strong a work'. The interior of this huge cylinder is awesome in its stark simplicity. The wooden floors have long since vanished, and the tower is thus open from the basement to the saucer-shaped stone dome by which it is roofed. Outside this dome runs the wall-walk, the battlements of which have loopholed merlons. There seems also to have been an upper parapet enclosing the dome. Putlog holes may still be seen for affixing a timber war-head. A single spiral stair serves the tower from basement to summit. The entrance is on the first floor, and was reached by a forestair, not applied to the tower, with which it was connected by a drawbridge. For its size and date, the domestic arrangments of this mighty donjon are surprisingly primitive. There are only two fireplaces, and no privies. Having regard to the marked early First Pointed character of the windows, we can hardly doubt that this astonishing tower was the work of William Marshal, the great Earl of Pembroke who stood by King John, not because he loved the man but because he dreaded a revival of the baronial anarchy in

Stephen's time, and who after the tyrant's death defeated the French invaders and on the infant King Henry's behalf renewed and improved the Great Charter. King Philip Augustus of France, against whom he gallantly but vainly defended Normandy, and who assuredly was no mean judge of character, described William Marshal as 'the most loyal man of his time'.

This imposing donjon presides over a broad array of curtain walls and round towers, enclosing a courtyard of nearly four acres. Towers and walls were badly shattered by Cromwell's guns and the subsequent demolitions, but since 1928 they have been progressively and sensitively restored, and the effect is splendid. Conspicuous is the rectangular gatehouse, which has twin staircase towers, two portcullises, and over the rearward portal a remarkable *blindage* or shield-wall carried on a great arch between the two towers, so as to form an embattled post for assailing, from above and in the rear, enemies who had succeeded in forcing the entrance as they emerged into the courtyard. This gatehouse is covered by a barbican, so arranged that the assailant must needs approach it with his right side, unprotected by a shield, exposed to missiles from an adjoining angle tower. On the other or left-hand side of the gatehouse, flanking defence is offered by a second tower on the curtain. The courtyard was divided by a cross wall, so as to form an outer and an inner ward. In the latter were two halls, a chapel and other domestic buildings. Of all these only fragments remain. Perhaps the most astonishing feature of this castle is the Wogan, a huge cavern excavated in the limestone at river level, and reached from the castle by a slippery spiral stair, the upper part of which is built, while the rest is 'hewn from the living rock profound'. This cavern has access from the water, and would serve as a store and boat-house. The origin of the name Wogan does not appear to be known, unless it be derived from John Wogan, an agent of the Earl of Pembroke in 1291.

The new fashion of round keeps came in just about the time when, as we shall see in a future chapter, the keep theme, whether round or square, was being discontinued in our English castles. There are, therefore, not many of these round keeps in the country. Most of them, for some reason, are in South Wales. One or two that may be mentioned are Caldicot, Longtown in Herefordshire and Skenfrith in Monmouthshire; Penrice in Gower, and Launceston in Cornwall; and Tretower in Brecknockshire. Each of these towers has its peculiarities, and only space prevents me from discussing them. Longtown and Skenfrith

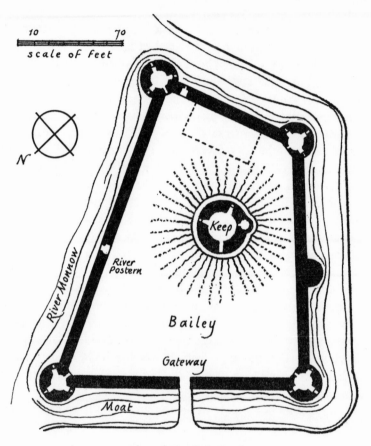

Plan of Skenfrith Castle

are remarkable for their semi-circular projections, breaking the outline of the cylinder. At Longtown there were three of these, one containing a privy and another a stair, while at Skenfrith the single projection likewise houses the stair. Launceston and Tretower are unusual in that they are each within a shell wall on top of a *motte*. At Launceston the shell wall is entire, and serves as a curtain to the tower. At Tretower the polygonal shell-keep, of Norman date, had been destroyed before the round tower was built: whether by hostile action, or as a prelude to building the latter, must remain uncertain.

5
Norman Town and Castle Planning

We have noted (p. 4) that church and castle, side by side, are the hallmarks of the Norman Conquest. Since castles tend to be placed at strategic points upon roads, and since such localities are likewise nodal points in trade communications, it is natural to find, all over the country, that towns have grown up under the shelter of a medieval castle. But in the frontier regions of England, over against the hostile Welsh and Scots, we find some of the most interesting cases of castles and dependent towns created contemporaneously, *d'un seul jet*, as it were—the town being designed as a garrison of soldier burgesses in the neighbourhood of a dangerous frontier. Some of these military boroughs display remarkable examples of purposeful town planning. Few more astonishing statements have ever been made by a distinguished medievalist than the late Professor Tout's dictum that in England no Norman boroughs 'give evidence of medieval town planning'. Let us take a brief look at two examples.

APPLEBY in Westmorland, new founded in a territory just won for the expanding Anglo-Norman realm, is in the strictest sense a colonial town. Its soldier burgesses were expected not only to promote civilisation amid the natives of a wild border district, but to defend it against the strong, aggressive Scotch kings of the Canmore dynasty. So its castle cannot be considered except in relation to the borough of which it was the nucleus. The lay-out of the borough and castle forms an articulated whole, the product of a standardised design, adapted to the site to which it has to be fitted.

The simplest type of medieval town may be described as the street market. This originated in the setting down of traders' booths or stock-pens at some convenient point on an arterial road. The resulting market town is aligned along an expansion of the road, like an elongated bubble blown on a glass tube. Both ends of this long market are equivalent. There is, so to speak, no polarisation of the market. This, the most primitive type of market town, can be illustrated by scores of examples throughout the length and breadth of England. The second type of market town is the product of a planned economy. A feudal motive supervenes. The castle of the lord of the manor, guaranteeing 'the peace of the market', forms the nucleus of the scheme, and the borough is laid out in dependence upon the castle. So the two ends of the street market are no longer equivalent. One end is polarised upon the castle of the superior. This is the plan of Appleby; and it is one of the most striking and attractive examples in feudal Europe.

In the mind of Ranulf de Meschines, the founder of Appleby, military considerations predominated. So he chose, for reasons of defence, the magnificent site enclosed by the 'incised meander' of the River Eden. On such a site of strong relief, the requirements of security and of commerce come into conflict. The military criterion is difficulty of access; the commercial criteria are smoothness of ground and easy approaches. At Appleby the military element was paramount, so the commercial convenience of the borough had to suffer. The castle was placed upon the loftiest part of the terrain, in the manner of an acropolis. The town stretched down into the river loop. So the lower end of the street market,which should have been the main inlet of trade, is hemmed in by the Eden. A solution of this difficulty was provided by the bridge. But in the choice of its site emerged a further complication. Room had also to be found, in the burghal *ensemble*, for the parish church and cemetery. On this constricted site, these could be placed nowhere else than in the apex of the loop, if the church and graveyard were not to compete for the valuable frontages on the market street. Hence the remarkable right-angled approach from the bridge to the market place, which is one of the arresting features in the town plan of Appleby.

The castle began as a mount-and-bailey stronghold of timbered earthwork, and its mighty banks and ditches survive as one of the most impressive examples of Norman military engineering in the country. In the twelfth century the *motte* was cut down, and on its truncated summit was built the fine late Norman stone keep that ever since has dominated the castle. On the whole, it seems most likely that this tower was built after the capture of Appleby by William the Lion in 1174. About the same time a curtain wall, afterwards strengthened by round towers, replaced the palisading of the bailey, and a Norman stone hall was erected at the far end of the bailey. How the castle fared in the Scotch wars we do not know, though the town was burned in 1314 and again in 1388. As part of a general programme of reorganising the frontier defences, the castles of Roger de Clifford, lord of Appleby, Brougham and Brough, were ordered to be repaired. Much building or rebuilding followed throughout the fifteenth century; but in 1539 the castle is described as ruinous, and the famous Lady Anne Clifford, who restored it in 1653, tells us that in the northern rebellion of 1569 its roofs were taken down, so as to leave 'no one chamber habitable'. Finally, between 1686 and 1688, the fourth Earl of Thanet built the existing east range, embodying the shell of its medieval predecessor. A further wing was added in 1695. This Restoration house is a fine essay in the pure neo-classical Renaissance. Later additions and alterations, while greatly improving the mansion as a comfortable modern re-sidence, have done nothing to impair its ancient features. So Appleby Castle stands today as an unrivalled pageant of military and domestic architecture from Norman times until the spacious days of the later Stuarts.

A close parallel to the lay-out of Appleby is provided, at the opposite end of the Scottish border, by another Norman castle and town, Warkworth in Northumberland (p. 34).

The third type of market town is the *bastide* or *ville neuve*, centrally planned round a market square. Castle and town are laid out simul-taneously as parts of one predetermined scheme. The town is disposed round a nuclear market place, with a regular gridiron pattern of street and housing blocks. This central plan is classically illustrated by the Edwardian boroughs of Snowdonia. But already we have instances of it in Norman and Angevin times. A good example is LUDLOW in Shropshire. Here castle and town, united in indissoluble marriage, form one of the most impressive, picturesque and historic complexes that have descended to us from Norman days. Its charm and interest

14 Bamburgh Castle

have never been set forth in more eloquent terms than by George T. Clark, in his time the foremost authority on our English castles:[1]

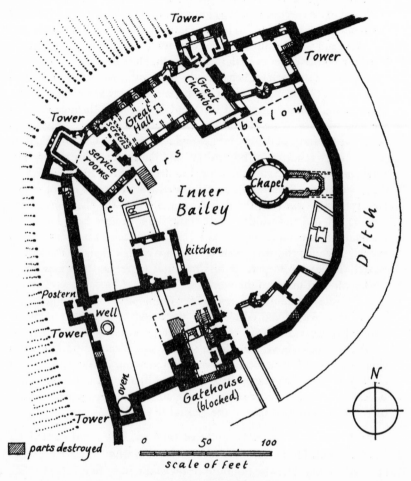

Plan of Ludlow Castle

Ludlow Castle is the glory of the middle marches of Wales, and first in place among the many military structures by which the great county of Salop has been adorned and defended. It is a noble specimen of military, palatial and even ecclesiastical architecture, of high antiquity and of

[1] *Medieval Military Architecture in England*, vol. II, pp. 273–90. The extract I have given is somewhat abridged.

15   Colchester Castle
16   *Ludlow Castle from the north*

historic fame. It is probably without rival in Britain for the sylvan beauty of its position, in which wood and water, and meadows of wide expanse and rare fertility, are combined with rugged and lofty crags, of which the walls and towers seem to form a component part. Nor are its associations with the past unworthy of so bright a scene. Here, in the age of chivalry, the Lacys and the Mortimers achieved many of those feats of arms which filled the border counties with their renown. Here Stephen exercised his great personal strength on behalf of the heir to the Scottish throne, who was about to be hauled up into the beleaguered castle by a somewhat uncouth and unusual engine of war; and against these formidable walls the wild tribes of Wales flung themselves for two centuries, only to fall back, like the surge of the sea, broken and scattered. The Castle of Ludlow was the early residence of Edward IV, and the cradle of his infant sons; and here died Prince Arthur, the elder brother of Henry VIII. In rather later times within these walls sat that celebrated Council of Wales of which Henry Sydney was long the President, and which the chambers of the building, ruined and roofless as they are, show to have been lodged so splendidly. Here too, towards the close of that brilliant but vicious provincial court, the attractions of which were felt even by the austere Baxter, Butler wrote part of his immortal satire, and the masque of *Comus* was first given to the world.

The Castle of Ludlow crowns a rocky promontory which projects at a height of above a hundred feet over the union of the Corve with the Teme. Eastward, and in its immediate rear, and rather lower than the castle but much above the adjacent plain, stands the grand cruciform church, with its lofty central tower, and about and below it the quaint old town. The town was walled, and its walls abutted upon the castle, which thus, as usual under such circumstances, though provided with its own defences, formed part of the general *enceinte*.

In his detailed and masterly study of Ludlow, town and castle,[1] Sir William St John Hope has pointed out that the town must have been laid out very soon after the building of the castle in its first form (which did not include the present outer ward) between 1085 and 1095. At first the town defences were doubtless palisading. Round the inside of them, for ease of access to a threatened point, ran a narrow lane, like the *intervallum* in a Roman fort. Stone walls and gates, of which considerable fragments remain, were added in the thirteenth century; these do not always follow the line of their timber predecessors. The interior

[1] *Archaeologia*, vol. LXI, pp. 257–328; 383–8.

of the town was regularly divided into blocks, like the *insulae* of a Roman city, by a gridiron of streets, of which the most important, the High Street, is polarised upon the castle. Much wider than the others, the High Street formed, as it still forms, the market stance. From Ludford Bridge it is approached at right angles, so that there is no direct access from the ancient bridge to the castle. As often in the Middle Ages, the great town church stands somewhat aloof from the street market, so as to preserve its dignity and sacred character from the 'stour' and sometimes the disorders of the market place—not to speak of the dust and stench with which the trafficking, to a large extent in livestock and provisions, was inevitably accompanied: in an apt phrase of Eric Linklater, 'the loud annoyance of an overcrowded market place'.

Organically united with the town, so that its curtain walls form an extension of the urban defences, and overlooking it down the market street, stands the noble castle. The outer ward, an early extension, forms a rough quadrangle: within it is the original castle, behind a wide, curving, rock-cut, dry ditch, which cuts off the north-western portion of the site, and in the rear abuts upon the steep rocky banks of the Teme. From the outer bailey—and of course originally, directly from the town—there is no straight entrance, any more than there is from the country to the town: for the mighty gatehouse tower stands well to the south in the curving line of the inner bailey. Originally this gatehouse was also the keep of the castle, after a fashion that (as we shall find) became common in later times. Later, as elsewhere, the inconvenience of this arrangement led to the blocking of the entrance through the keep and the opening of a new gateway on the north side. Still later, the keep was reduced in dimensions on the courtyard side. It is beyond the scope of this book to offer a description of the numerous and stately lodgings which surround the inner bailey. Mostly they belong to the fourteenth century, but were much altered, embellished and extended in Tudor times. Space, however, must be found for a word about the richly decorated Norman chapel of St. Mary Magdalene, with its circular nave, like the Temple Church in London, or the Romanesque church of Orphir in the remote Orkney Islands. Such churches, of which about half a dozen survive in Britain, and other nine are known to have existed, were modelled upon the Church of the Holy Sepulchre in Jerusalem.

With its narrow streets, sometimes cobble-margined, its picturesque half-timbered frontages dating from late medieval and Tudor times, its fine Jacobean and Georgian mansions, and high over all the noble Perpendicular tower of St Lawrence's Church, Ludlow town and its splendid castle afford us an unrivalled conspectus of English burghal life from the Norman Conquest to the present century, which has seen a new and thriving extension growing up outside the medieval walls. And if you are so lucky as to be there on a market day, then the animated picturesqueness of the varied stalls and the motley, chaffering multitude takes us right back into the Middle Ages—were it not for the parked vehicles and the all-pervading reek of petrol.

6

Castles of Enceinte

Comparatively few cylindrical donjons exist in England and Wales, for the simple reason that the conception of the donjon, whether round or square, was in course of being abandoned about the turn of the twelfth century. In peace, the inconvenience of a lofty tower, with its living rooms piled on top of each other, requires no expounding; while in war, its inefficiency as a *dernier ressort* had been demonstrated by many famous sieges—notably that of Château Gaillard in Normandy, where the garrison, once the three baileys had been successively wrested from them, surrendered without any attempt to defend their stupendous donjon. Experience has shown that the multiplication of defences, however awkward for the attacking force, was likewise inconvenient for the defenders, whom these intricate obstacles prevented from moving rapidly to a menaced part of the castle. A process of general simplification of the castle theme now emerges. Reliance was placed upon a single wall of *enceinte*, well defended by skilfully posted round flanking towers, to no one of which a special importance was assigned. The large single internal courtyard thus provided permitted a far more convenient scheme for the residential quarters, disposed now horizontally, and planned upon the ampler and more luxurious scale demanded by the rapidly expanding requirements of a baronial household in the opulent thirteenth century.

The new type of castle is perfectly illustrated by one of the most attractive, historical, architecturally interesting, and least-known of British castles, MANORBIER on the Pembrokeshire coast. In medieval literature this castle is famous as the birthplace (about 1146) of Gerald de Barry, in Latin known as Giraldus Cambrensis, Gerald of Wales, whose *Itinerary through Wales, Topography of Ireland,* and *Conquest of Ireland,* all written in elegant Latin, place him in the front rank of medieval historians. In the *Rolls* series, his works make up no less than eight volumes. Son of the Norman lord of Manorbier, he had Welsh blood in his veins, spoke the Welsh language, and in all his writings presents himself proudly as a Welsh patriot. In one of the round towers of Manorbier Castle you are astonished to find a room furnished in the fashion of the twelfth century, containing a life-sized wax effigy of Gerald of Wales, sitting at his desk and busily engaged in writing one of the books that have given him an enduring place among scholars of his native Wales. The castle consists of a spacious oblong courtyard, lying more or less east and west, with a forecourt on the eastern or entrance front. This front is flanked at either end by two large round towers, more or less equal in size. Otherwise the massive and lofty curtain wall is not provided with towers, which indeed are hardly necessary, since the castle occupies the whole of a promontory defined by very steep slopes. In the centre of the foreface is an oblong gatehouse, boldly projected and provided with the usual defences. In the portcullis room, the ancient windlass remains above the slot, with the wheels at either end required to manhandle it. The stubs of the spokes or handles may be seen in each wheel. In the two round towers the stairs curve up in the thickness of the wall, and each successive flight opens on the opposite side of the room from its predecessor, so that persons ascending have to cross each floor of the tower in turn. We have already noted this security device in the Conisbrough donjon.

Along the south side and west end of the courtyard is arranged an extensive but well articulated suite of living rooms. The principal apartments are on the west, and comprise a hall on the first floor, with solar above, private rooms at one end and a chapel at the other. The chapel has a pointed barrel vault. Both chapel and hall are reached by forestairs. Between them a passage leads to a postern in the west curtain. In the main these domestic buildings, which are well fitted up and finely detailed, seem to date from about 1300; but they have been much altered at various periods. A portion of them, towards the east, has been remodelled as a habitable house. Externally the long array of battlemented walls on their commanding stance, makes a most imposing effect, and the front, with its central square gatehouse and round flanking towers, speaks to us in no uncertain terms about the stern

reality of feudal power. On this front, the castle is isolated by a wide
dry ditch from a walled forecourt of which one round tower in part
remains. In this forecourt are the ruins of a long building, part barn and
stable. Inside the main court, the curtain walls are bordered with well-
tended flower beds. Giraldus speaks of his birthplace with filial pride:

> The castle is conspicuous by its towers and ramparts, and stands on the
> summit of a slope which stretches towards the harbour on the west. To
> the north and north-west it has an enormous fish-pond, right under the
> walls, notable as much for its size as for the depth of its waters, and a
> most beautiful park on the same side. This in its turn is enclosed by a
> vineyard at one end, and at the other by a glade distinguished both by
> its jutting rocks and its tall hazel trees.

Another fine example of the new, simplified type of castle is FRAM-
LINGHAM in Suffolk. Here, the flanking towers, thirteen in all, are of the
old-fashioned rectangular plan. Moreover, most of them are open to
the interior, and thus are no longer conceived as independent defensible
posts, which, if captured by an enemy, could easily be held against the
garrison in the courtyard. The old military principle, 'that which
defends must itself be defended', is here boldly discarded. Two of the
towers have solid bases: in the towers generally, there will have been
wooden fronts towards the courtyard, and as they rise high above the
curtains, the wall-walks were reached from the upper floors of the
towers. One tower is set aside to house the single spiral stair by which the
wall-walk was reached. Framlingham Castle began its career as what
may be described as a 'ring and bailey'; for what ought to have been
the *motte*, an area measuring about 250 feet by 200, is not raised at all,
or very little, above the general ground level. The bailey is large and
kidney shaped, lapping round the south and east of the central enclosure, or *Kernburg*—to borrow a handy German term. To the north-
west there is also a 'lower court', as it is described in old writings. The
whole complex is enclosed by formidable banks and ditches, and was
further secured upon the western front by a broad mere. To the south-
west lies the bright little market town, dominated by the stately
Perpendicular church, with its Howard tombs; and the town ditch was
carried out and round to enclose the precinct of the castle.

Although the interior buildings of the *Kernburg* have long been
removed, the great array of walls and towers survives practically
intact, and provides us with one of the most impressive displays of

medieval fortification in England. The main entrance fronts the town, and the ditch here is spanned by a single-arched Tudor bridge of stone and brick; but the piers below are medieval. In front of this bridge, over against the town, there was formerly a *lunette*. The bridge replaces a timber structure, resting on the piers aforesaid, and connected with the gatehouse by a drawbridge. The gatehouse, square like all the other towers, was defended by a portcullis and folding gates. Over the portal are displayed the arms of the Howard Dukes of Norfolk. Within the castle, on the eastern side, were the earliest hall and chapel: but about the year 1200 the former was replaced on the opposite side by a new hall, some fragments of which can be made out in the picturesque seventeenth-century gabled and mullioned almshouse which now occupies this site. The masonry of the castle is highly distinctive, being 'small-work' of flint, regularly coursed, with carefully dressed freestone quoins; but there is much later patching in brick. The curtain walls are 44 feet high and 8 feet thick, and above them the towers rise a further 14 feet or thereby. An amusing feature of the profile is provided by the tall array of variously ornamented Tudor chimneys in cut brick. Most of these are bogus—built purely for effect. In the curtain wall are two posterns. One is on the north-east, and led out across the ditch by a timber bridge, resting on six slender piers. The other is on the west side, and admits to a covered way, solidly walled with stone and loopholed on either side, so as to flank the southern end of the ditch in the manner of a *caponier*. This passage conducts to the prison tower, from which a short length of wall completes the closing of the ditch, ending at the mound of the lower bailey. A similar wall, also provided with a square tower, closes the northern end of the ditch. The broad bank of the lower court never seems to have been walled, though it exhibits the slender foundations of buildings doubtless late in date.

The site of Framlingham Castle has been occupied since very early times; for a Saxon cemetery, dating apparently from the seventh and eighth centuries, was found in the outer bailey, in front of the main entrance. Henry I gave Framlingham to Roger Bigod, whose son Hugh was created first Earl of Norfolk (or East Anglia as the title then went). Roger seems to have laid out the first castle of timbered earthwork, while the original hall on the east side may be ascribed to his son. Henry II, against whom Hugh Bigod had rebelled at least twice,

17   *Pembroke Castle*
18   *Barnwell Castle*

dismantled the timber castle in 1175. The existing masonry castle was the work of his son, the second Earl, about the turn of the twelfth century. In the Magna Carta struggle the castle was besieged and won by King John. Apart from a short interval of royal ownership under Edward I, Framlingham continued to be held by the various baronial houses—Brothertons, Mowbrays and Howards—who enjoyed the proud dignity of Dukes of Norfolk. About the middle of the sixteenth century it ceased to be regularly occupied: but the crowning moment of its history came in 1553, when Mary Tudor, to whom Framlingham had been granted by her brother Edward VI, retired to the castle and called her supporters to her aid against the usurpation of Lady Jane Gray. Round its walls a large army gathered, but before it could move against London the rebellion had collapsed. To Framlingham thereafter came Nicholas Ridley, Bishop of London, to sue for pardon. Considering that he had publicly proclaimed, in a sermon preached before a disapproving congregation in St Paul's Cathedral, that the Queen was a bastard, it was hardly to be expected, the spirit of the times being what it was, that his plea for mercy could find favour. He was at once arrested and sent off to the Tower: and it is a matter of history how in due course, with his colleague Latimer, Bishop of Worcester, he submitted with heroic constancy to a cruel and lingering martyr's death outside the walls of Balliol College, Oxford (16 October 1555).

In 1636 Sir Robert Hitcham, the owner of Framlingham, bequeathed it to Pembroke College, Cambridge, of which at one time Ridley had been master. In accordance with the testator's wishes the interior buildings were demolished, and replaced by the existing almshouse, now used for county purposes. In 1913 the Master and Fellows of Pembroke College handed over the castle to the then Commissioners of Works, by whom thereafter the ruins were put into repair.

BARNWELL CASTLE in Northamptonshire, built about 1266, shows us very clearly the stage of development at which the English castle had arrived by the second half of the thirteenth century, when the weakness of the donjon theme, to which I have already alluded, had been demonstrated by practical experience. This castle has been well described as 'a good example of the type of stronghold erected when the strengthening of outer walls and entrances had made the keep superfluous and the defence of the curtains had made necessary the multiplication of flanking towers'. It also illustrates another influence which now was making itself felt in the design of castles. This was the urge towards symmetry so characteristic of the classical spirit that marked the thirteenth century. It is worth considering this matter for a moment: since castles must not be regarded too strictly from the standpoint of 'military architecture', and other considerations besides the laws of fortification and the progress of siegecraft have played a part in their design.

The noble thirteenth century saw the climax of medieval civilisation. In spite of all the Nordic elements successively contributed to it since the catastrophe of the Roman Empire, that civilisation remained essentially a Latin one. In this culminating era of the High Middle Ages —when, in the words of John Richard Green, 'the long mental in-activity of feudal Europe broke up like ice before a summer's sun', and a new humanism permeated the western nations—it was natural that men's minds should become more and more conscious of the debt which they owed to old Rome, and should seek inspiration, as they had not done for centuries past, from Latin models in art and literature. In literature, we have already noted an early example of this medieval pre-figuration of the Renaissance in the writings of Gerald de Barry at Manorbier. In the realm of building, from the wilfulness and irregular-ity of Dark Age planning in town and castle, men turned again to the symmetry and the noble harmonies that had marked the architecture of classical antiquity. So we find, in southern France, the revival of town planning, after the old Roman pattern, in the *bastides or villes neuves* of which I have already spoken, founded both by French and English—fortified towns, such as Aigues-Mortes or Montpazier, which reproduce the rigid rectangular lay-out of streets and the central forum of a Roman *colonia*. Edward I introduced the new idea into England at Hull and Winchester, and into Wales in the walled towns which he attached to his castles. We have seen that town planning was not un-known in Norman England; but not until the reign of Edward I, a notable town planner both in Aquitaine and in Britain, do we find the fully developed *ville neuve* with its street gridiron converging on a central forum. Far away in East Prussia, and along the track of German settlers high up into the wilds of Livonia, we see the same rectilinear colonial towns springing up, a witness to the neo-classical spirit of the

thirteenth century. This new love of symmetry and classical completeness invaded also the realm of church architecture, then mounting
to its highest achievements. The great Gothic cathedrals, Rheims and
Amiens, Notre-Dame in Paris, Strasbourg and Naumburg, Siena,
Canterbury and Salisbury, show the same striving after symmetry and
rhythmical order in all their parts. The grouping and proportion of their
windows, the bays of choir and nave and transepts, are designed upon
an exact geometrical system of multiples of units. '*Li ars de iometrie le
commande et ensaigne*'—the art of geometry biddeth and teacheth—so

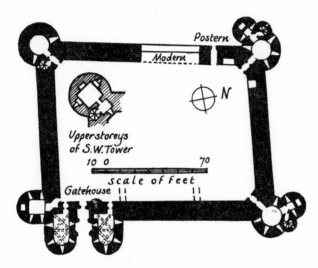

Plan of Barnwell Castle

wrote Villard de Honnecourt, a great architect of the time; and his
own sketch book shows how geometrical schemes and ideas of symmetry governed everything, even representations of birds and beasts
and of the human face and figure. Small wonder, therefore, that the
same passion for balance and classical completeness manifests itself also
in the castles of the century.

Of this new passion for symmetry Barnwell Castle is an early and
striking example. On plan it is a simple rectangle, enclosed by thick and
lofty curtain walls. At all four angles are bold round towers. The in-
creasing attention now being devoted to these features is revealed in the
remarkable design of the two northern towers, which form triple

segments of cylinders, the central and smallest one containing a spiral stair, while of the other two the larger one provides good living rooms, and the smaller contains the privies. On the east side, at the south end, and associated with the south-east angle tower which therefore projects only to the south, is the gatehouse. This is still no more than an entrance passage between two drum towers, and displays none of the special features afterwards developed in the great Edwardian 'keep-gatehouses', which we shall have to consider in our next chapter. Thus the three successive doors in the entrance passage all close outwards. The inner-most one does not shut against the courtyard, as became the fashion in the Edwardian gatehouses, nor is there a rear portcullis. The basement of the gatehouse is all vaulted. It never seems to have had more than two floors, of which the upper one contained the portcullis chamber over the entrance passage, with apartments in the towers. There is no sign yet of the large residential hall which became characteristic of the Edwardian keep-gatehouse. A notable feature is the narrowness of the rear portal, which is no more than 4 feet 9 inches wide. It can have ad-mitted no wheeled traffic; and the existence of an outer court is proved by earthworks. The buildings inside the courtyard have all been des-troyed. But the great hall was on the east side, with its gable against the curtain—no very convenient arrangement. Probably therefore these buildings were of a somewhat incoherent or unarticulated description. A notable feature of this remarkable castle is the double crosslet loop-holes—one long slit with two short transverse slits. The curtain walls are 12 feet thick and 30 feet high: the courtyard area, not a perfect rect-angle, measures about 125 feet by 95 feet.

The multiple northern towers of Barnwell Castle are most peculiar. Undoubtedly they portray the mood of busy experimental inventiveness that possessed castle builders in the middle years of the thirteenth century.

An earlier castle at Barnwell is vouched for by the prominent earth-works of a mount and bailey, very irregularly formed, a short distance to the north-west of the stone ruin. The latter was built by Berenger le Moyne; later owners were the family of Montagu. The fine Elizabethan mansion adjoining, with its charming array of broad gables and tall chimneys, is now the seat of T.R.H. The Duke and Duchess of Glou-cester: and the interior of the old castle has been laid out as a tennis court.

Leaving for the next chapter consideration of the great Edwardian fortresses with their characteristic keep-gatehouses, we pursue the study of the simple keepless castle, symmetrically planned, of later Plantagenet times.

BODIAM CASTLE was built, pursuant to a royal licence granted on 20 October 1385, by the famous knight Sir Edward Dallingrigge, a veteran of the third Edward's continental wars. The licence empowers him 'to strengthen with a wall of stone and lime, and crenellate and construct and make into a castle his manor of Bodyham, near the sea, in the county of Sussex, for defence of the adjacent country and resistance to our enemies'. The motive prompting the grant, so clearly revealed in this language, is illustrated by the fact that eight years previously, owing to the paralytic condition of the English navy in the decadent closing days of Edward III, a French fleet under the great Admiral Jean de Vienne, whose exploits adorn the brilliant pages of Froissart, had sacked the port of Rye. In fact, between Pembroke's defeat off La Rochelle in 1372 and Arundel's victory at Margate two years after the Bodiam licence, England had lost control of the Channel. The eighties of the fourteenth century were a decade of great strain and alarm. Plantagenet imperialism had already committed the realm to a war upon two fronts, against France and Scotland; and now the policy of the Black Prince, in supporting Pedro the Cruel in Spain, followed as it was by John of Gaunt's dynastic venture in that country, added the naval powers of Castile to the hostile array. The resultant alliance of Valois, Stewart, and Trastamara all but brought the weak government of Richard II to its knees. The Franco-Castilian fleet swept the Channel and occupied the Isle of Wight. English ports from Hastings to Scarborough were given to the flames. Up in the north, in 1385, a French fleet arrived in the Forth and landed troops to take a hand in the Scots invasions which year after year were scourging the miserable border lands. Under such conditions of peril, the English government embarked on a comprehensive programme of strengthening and reconditioning the existing frontier and coastal defences, and building new castles when required. Thus Bodiam Castle was not merely the private stronghold of a feudal baron. It was intended to be in some sense a national fortalice, and required a standing garrison. This would be ready to hand in the numerous veterans of the French war—'free companions' such as are so vividly portrayed in Sir Arthur Conan

Doyle's novels, *The White Company* and *Sir Nigel*. No longer was it a question of the feudal lord calling up his tenantry to defend his residence in time of need. For a standing garrison special accommodation had to be provided; and as these hard-boiled mercenaries were liable to be awkward neighbours, their quarters must be carefully isolated from

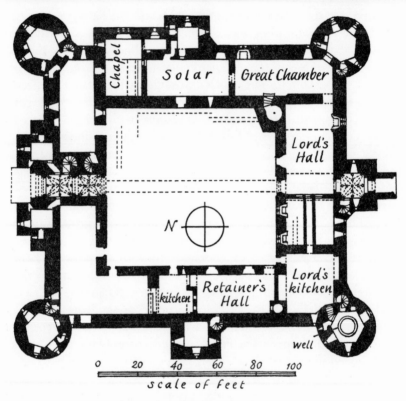

Plan of Bodiam Castle

those of the lord of the castle and his household. We shall see how admirably the design of Bodiam Castle has been adjusted to meet these novel requirements.

On looking at the plan, it will be seen that the buildings on the southern and eastern sides of the courtyard, and on the north side east of the gatehouse, form a connected suite of intercommunicating apartments, providing a complete residence which consists, as we proceed counter-clockwise round the quadrangle, of kitchen, buttery and pantry, hall, great chamber, solar apartments, and chapel. The buildings on the west side of the courtyard, and in the western half of the northern side, likewise form a self-contained suite, and are furnished with a second hall and a second kitchen. Obviously these were set aside for the retainers, while the rest of the buildings were apportioned to the lord's *mesnie* or household. Note that the retainers' quarters are completely isolated. They communicate neither with the gatehouse at their one end nor with the lord's suite at the other. It is significant that the water-supply in the south-west tower is under the lord's control. So is the gatehouse, which is secured equally against foes without and disorder within. Note also the special security given to the south-east tower. It alone has a vaulted basement; and in it alone the stair can be reached only by entering the tower—elsewhere, entrance to the towers is obtained through the stairs. Hence this south-eastern tower, opening off the private apartments, possesses something of the character of the donjon in a thirteenth-century castle.

Bodiam Castle stands within a wide moat, of dimensions large enough to be termed an artificial lake. The approaches to the castle, in front and rear, are of very high interest. Opposite the main gate on the northern side an octagonal stone-cased island is formed in the midst of the water, and this was reached at right-angles by a bridge from the west bank, and by a second bridge connecting with the gatehouse. Thus an enemy seeking to approach the portal must expose his right flank, unprotected by a shield. The south gate, or postern, communicates by a third bridge with a small harbour, excavated in the bank of the Rother, which in the fourteenth century was here a navigable river.

Lord Curzon, who bought this noble ruin, repaired it, and bequeathed it to the nation, rightly describes Bodiam as 'the most fairy of English castles'. Its grey old walls and round or square towers, and the two frowning machicolated gatehouses, all sheerly emergent from the broad tranquil waters of the lake, stand forth against a background of green slopes and ancient trees. The lake itself is carpeted with masses of water lilies, expanding in the season their great white or yellow blossoms. It is the haunt of the kingfisher and the shy little dab-chick, and white swans sail in conscious majesty upon the open reaches of the water.

A close and contemporary parallel to Bodiam is furnished by the north

country at BOLTON CASTLE in Wensleydale. The licence to build it was
granted by Richard II to his Chancellor, Richard, Lord Scrope, on 4
July 1379. Evidently its erection was part of the general policy of
strengthening frontier and coastal defences which I have already
mentioned. According to Leland, the work of building went on for

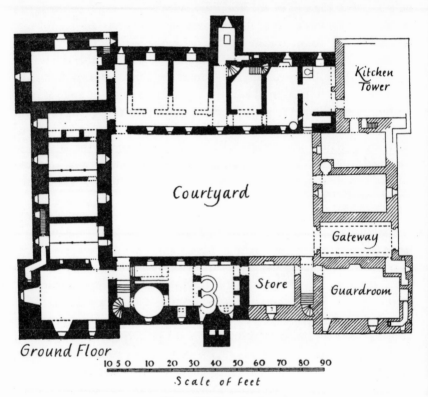

Plan of Bolton Castle

eighteen years, at an annual cost of 1000 marks. An interesting feature
connected with the undertaking is the survival of the contract between
Lord Scrope and the great northern architect, John Lewyn, dated
14 September 1378. The work that Lewyn undertook to build is clearly
specified, and recognisable in the fabric today. It consisted of the north-
eastern or kitchen tower; the gatehouse, including the south-eastern
tower that adjoins it; and the contiguous part of the south wing, as far
west as the chapel gable. Although all this was built as a unit, in terms

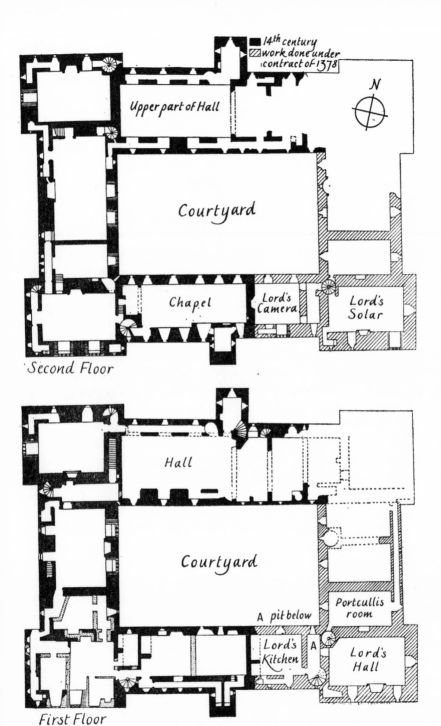

■ 14th century
▨ work done under
contract of 1378

N

Upper part of Hall

Courtyard

Chapel   Lord's Camera   Lord's Solar

Second Floor

Hall

Courtyard

A pit below

Portcullis room

Lord's Kitchen   A   Lord's Hall

First Floor

of the indenture, it is obvious that the whole castle follows a uniform design, and I have little doubt that John Lewyn was the master-mason of the entire structure. Also it is obvious that the work contracted for in 1378 was the final stage in the erection of the castle, which will have been built from the west eastward, so as to leave the accessible side, or entrance front, open as long as possible for the introduction of building materials. It therefore follows that, as so often, the erection of the castle was begun in anticipation of the royal licence.

Like Bodiam, Bolton Castle forms a symmetrical rectangular structure, enclosing an oblong courtyard, with towers at the four angles and midway in each long face. Only at Bolton the northern fashion of square towers is followed throughout. Situated in a disturbed border district, and clearly designed to house a standing garrison of professional soldiery, the building exhibits all the special provision for security that we found at Bodiam. The entrance passage was defended by a portcullis at either end: moreover, all five doorways which admit into the interior buildings were likewise furnished with portcullises, and the four corner doors are further defended by a machicolated jutty overhead. Thus maximum security was provided, not only against an enemy who had forced his way into the courtyard, but also against any trouble from the standing garrison of free-lances.

The entire south-east quarter of the castle, comprising the gatehouse, the south-eastern tower, and the part betwixt the latter and the chapel, forms a self-contained building, carefully shut off, on every floor, from the rest of the edifice—save only for one narrow door in the basement connecting with the bakehouse beyond, against which this door closed, and was secured by a stout drawbar. We can hardly fail to recognise, in this self-contained structure, the residence of the lord or castellan, frontally sited, and with the castle entrance under his control. On the ground floor, it contains the entance passage, a guard-room (with capacious fireplace) in the south-east tower, and a cellar to the west. The first floor, reached by a passage and spiral stair from the door in the south-east corner of the courtyard, contains the lord's hall in the tower, a separate kitchen for his *familia* on the west, and the portcullis room over the entrance passage to the north. This last room, so vital to the safety of the place, is given exceptional security. It is reached only from above, by a newel stair descending from the castellan's solar, which occupies the second floor of the south-east tower, with his *camera* adjoining to the west. Between these two rooms is a narrow apartment, in the floor of which is a trap door, giving access to a vaulted cell below. The whole forms the sort of provision for captives familiar in contemporary Scottish castles, where we often find an upper room for prisoners whom it is desired to treat with some consideration, while below is a 'pit' for those consigned to durance vile. Thus the lord or constable could retain any prisoners in his own custody, while in the north mid-tower another prison was provided for more general use. The rest of the castle, like Bodiam, contains on its main floor a complete articulated suite of apartments deployed counter-clockwise round the quadrangle, beginning with the common kitchen in the north-east tower, followed in succession by butteries and pantry; great hall, great chamber in the north-west tower; solar, guest rooms in the south-west tower; and a fine large chapel in the south range. Beneath all were the usual offices.

Bolton Castle is famous as the prison, from 15 July 1568, of Mary Queen of Scots, until 26 January following, when, upon the threatened outbreak of the great northern Catholic revolt against Elizabeth, it was deemed prudent to remove the royal captive to the safer distance of Tutbury. About Bolton Castle Sir Francis Knollys thus reported to Queen Elizabeth:

> This house appeareth to be very strong, very fair, and very stately, after the old manner of building; and is the highest-walled house that I have seen, and hath but one entrance thereinto; and half the number of soldiers may better watch and ward the same than the whole number thereof could do at Carlisle Castle.

Space permits us to consider no more than a final example of the symmetrically planned keepless castles which are typical of late fourteenth-century military construction. FARLEIGH HUNGERFORD CASTLE in Somerset was built in the thirteen-seventies by Sir Thomas Hungerford, the first recorded Speaker of the House of Commons—a merchant prince and Chief Steward of John of Gaunt's lands south of Trent. The work was doubtless more or less completed by 1383, when Sir Thomas received a royal pardon for undertaking it without the necessary licence. We can hardly doubt that this, like Bodiam, is another case of fortifying the realm against overseas invasion: for Farleigh lies in a rich country, easily accessible both from the Severn and from the Channel. It is significant that in 1346 the inhabitants of Somerset were exempted from service in the Crécy campaign, so that they should be available to repel a French landing. And even Oxford, in 1378, was ordered to strengthen its defences against the danger of a French invasion.

The situation chosen by Sir Thomas is one of considerable strength. To the north it backs upon the steep bank of Dane's Dyke, a small tributary of the River Frome, while on either flank, east and west, are natural scarps. The eastern slope is the bank of the Frome: the western appears to have been artificially deepened, and dammed with masonry to form a storage pond. The enclosure was completed by a cross ditch on the south; and within the rectangular area thus defined Sir Thomas Hungerford laid out his castle upon a four-square plan, with a cylindrical tower at each angle and in the middle of the fore-face a simple gatehouse of two rectangular towers with circled fronts. Rather unusually, the great hall, with its kitchen and offices at the west end and the lord's apartments at the other, straddles the courtyard, dividing it into two parts, of which the smaller or north portion contained a bakehouse and a kitchen garden. One suspects that the domestic lay-out, thus abnormally sited, may be inherited from a previous manor-house: there is an unauthenticated record of a 'castle' at Farleigh having been burnt in 1342. Unfortunately the interior buildings have been demolished, while the outer walls and towers are sorely ruined. Only the two southern towers now bulk large in the general aspect of the castle.

Outside the fore-face stood the original parish church of Farleigh, dedicated to St Leonard. It appears to have been entirely rebuilt by Sir Thomas Hungerford: yet its close association with the castle smacks of Norman arrangements, and seems to confirm the idea that there was an earlier castle, or manor-house, upon the site. Support is lent to this conjecture by the survival of a twelfth-century font in the chapel. Early in the fifteenth century, his son, Sir Walter Hungerford, a famous soldier under Henry V, and sometime Treasurer of England, enlarged the castle, forming a forecourt so as to take in the parish church. Henceforth this served as the lord's private chapel, and a new parish church, likewise dedicated to St Leonard, was built by Sir Walter, and consecrated in 1443. The fifteenth-century forecourt, enclosed by a deep and wide ditch, is of irregular shape, defended by round towers and provided with a simple square gatehouse and a postern at the north-west corner, covered by the south-western tower of the original castle.

Upon the north side of the former parish church Sir Thomas Hungerford had added a chantry chapel, dedicated to St Anne; and a west porch was built in the early sixteenth century. The church, which is still roofed and fitted up now as a museum, is a structure of much interest. It formed the burial place of the Hungerfords, and contains five family tombs, including that of Sir Thomas Hungerford and his lady. Underneath St Anne's Chapel is a vaulted crypt, in which are eight leaden coffins, two of them being those of children. Four of these coffins have faces moulded upon them. Unfortunately they have been desecrated, nor is it known to which members of the family they belonged. Close east of the church site is the priest's house, built in 1430, and though much altered, still inhabited.

Of course the effigy of the first Speaker of the Commons is of exceptional interest. The face is evidently a portrait: and the likeness reappears in a stained glass medallion of Sir Thomas Hungerford, now in the present parish church. This stained glass portrait of the old knight is one of the most delightful things of its kind in all England. It is obviously a 'speaking likeness'. We see Sir Thomas with his pouchy eyes, strongly beaked nose, fierce pendant moustaches, and peppery expression. It shows how early the standard type of the English country squire had become fixed. We picture the good knight sitting over his wine, cursing those scoundrelly peasants who had revolted against their lawful masters, railing at the imbecility of the government, and lamenting the brave old days of the French war, in which, profiteering from high prices and low wages, he had doubtless amassed the wealth that he had expended in creating his stately castle.

Excavated, conserved, and tastefully laid out by the Ministry of Public Building and Works, Farleigh Hungerford is now one of the most interesting castles in the West Country.

7

Master James of St George and The Edwardian Castles

In the last chapter we have followed the story of the simplified, symmetrically planned keepless castles, introduced about the year 1200, down to the time when they passed out of current fashion towards the end of the fourteenth century. Long before that time, however, a new and more formidable type of castle had come into being. This is characterised by a concentric arrangement of wards, and by the substitution of the older keep, construed mainly in terms of passive defence, and often placed in the least accessible part of the enceinte, by a frontally sited and much more aggressively planned structure, combining the functions of keep, gatehouse, and quarters for the lord or castellan. This new type of building, which marks the climax of English castellar construction, is prominently associated with the fortresses built by Edward I to secure his conquest of Wales, and with the name of his architect, James of St George, the foremost master of castle-building in medieval England.

Master James of St George was brought into England, and into the service of Edward I, from Savoy. He was not the inventor of the concentric castle; nor, as we shall shortly find, did he always build his castles upon a concentric design. The theme of the concentric castle was borrowed by western military engineers from Syria and the Levant, where the Crusades had introduced them to the grand fortresses of the Byzantine Empire, in which the concentric principle had descended in unbroken continuity from Roman times. The idea of opposing successive wards, or defensive envelopes, to an attacker was no new one, even in the West. It is fully displayed at Château Gaillard, built by Coeur-de-Lion about 1196–8. But in the true concentric castle the inner envelope is wholly enclosed by the outer; and as the latter is always much lower the two can be in action against an assailant at the same time. In this simultaneous activation of the entire defensive resources of the garrison lay a major part of the special strength of such castles. The Crusading engineers were quick to grasp the fact, and already in the first quarter of the thirteenth century we have a completely concentric castle at Le Krak des Chevaliers in Syria. The town of Carcassonne in Provence, refortified in the latter half of the century, illustrates the arrival of the new concept in the West. In England, the Tower of London, as reorganised by Henry III and Edward I, is a perfect example of a concentric castle.

On the other hand the keep-gatehouse appears to be a distinctively English invention. We have seen that in the castles of the earlier part of the thirteenth century the donjon or keep is usually at the back or remotest corner of the *enceinte*, as far removed as possible from the point of greatest danger; and that its power of resistance was in the main a passive one—in fact, it was conceived as a *dernier ressort*, into which the garrison might retire, if they could, should the rest of the castle be taken. By contrast, in the keep-gatehouse the weight and mass of the castle is brought forward and frontally concentrated. The lord's or governor's residence is combined with the gatehouse, in the forefront of the fight, and the commandant has the drawbridge, portcullises, and other defences of the entrance passage under his immediate personal control—an important safeguard at this period, when the feudal lords were relying less and less upon their own vassals and more and more upon paid retainers, whose fidelity was often doubtful. Small garrisons of hired professional soldiers were now the rule; and distrust of these mercenaries is revealed by the fact that in the typical keep-gatehouse the portcullis, folding doors, and other defences are duplicated in the rear of the entrance passage, but arranged so as to close *against* the castle courtyard.

The first castle built by Master James of St George in North Wales was not devised upon the concentric scheme. In fact it was built upon a plan never afterwards repeated in Britain. FLINT CASTLE, commenced in 1277, has always puzzled archaeologists. Having failed to understand it, they have often sought refuge in abusing it. The offending structure has been roundly dismissed as an anachronism, an 'inadequate plan', a piece of useless ingenuity, a castle whose two portions 'are not only not mutually helpful, but are so constituted as to be sources of danger to each other'—in a word, a thing that failed of its purpose and for this reason was never copied. More recent criticism has recognised in Flint

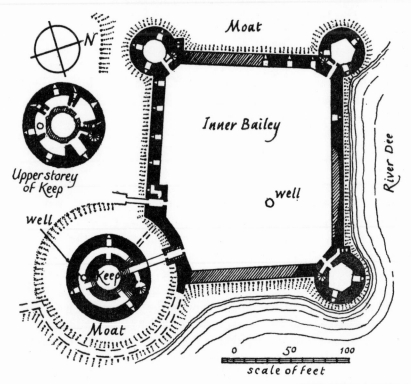

Plan of Flint Castle

Castle an exceptionally able design by an engineer of great resource, who knew exactly what he wanted to do—even if his *tour-de-force* was superseded almost at once by the more dynamic theme of the keep-gatehouse.

Briefly summarised, Flint Castle consists of a rectangular enclosure screened by thick and lofty curtain walls, having a strong round tower at each corner, of which one is much larger than the rest and formed the keep or donjon. To this main castle was added an entrenched fore-

court communicating with the timbered earthwork defences of the borough—the latter being regularly designed as a *bastide* or *ville anglaise*, of the type which King Edward built in Aquitaine.

So far, this may seem to be a somewhat old-fashioned plan; for by 1277 the donjon was becoming an obsolescent feature in the castle scheme. Yet be it noted that the keep at Flint is placed not in the rear but in the front face of the castle, dominating the forecourt and the *bastide* beyond, as well as the harbour. Also it is completely isolated from the main castle by a moat, into which the sea was admitted, and which was spanned by a drawbridge. In these two respects, our tower at Flint has been anticipated, half a century before, by the noblest of all cylindrical donjons, the mighty keep of the Château de Coucy, wantonly destroyed by the Germans in the First World War: *un donjon tel que le monde n'en a vu et n'en verra jamais de semblable*, to quote the lament of a leading French authority. Other examples exist in France of this propugnacular position of the donjon, which also is met with in some German and Scandinavian castles of the thirteenth century.

The ground floor of the Flint donjon is arranged in an extraordinary way. Its inner chamber is comparatively small, and is surrounded by a mural gallery, circling the immense thickness (23 feet) of the tower wall, and stepped down, and then up again, so as to dive under the entrance passage of the donjon, with which passage it does not communicate. This gallery is entered by three doors and steps down into the central chamber, whereunto the entrance passage likewise has descending steps. The gallery has no parallel on the first floor of the donjon, which was normally arranged, containing a large hall with mural chambers, one of which was the chapel, and another seemingly the kitchen. To this first floor access is obtained by a spiral stair, opening from the entrance passage in the usual way. Nothing now remains of upper storeys; and indeed it appears that the donjon was not completed until 1302, and then only in timber work, which included a 'beautiful circular gallery' —presumably an overhanging *bretasche* or defensive hoarding. Stonework was fitted into the tower 'for receiving and sustaining the said woodwork'. Doubtless this implies a series of corbels to support the *bretasche*, after the fashion of the time.

What is the meaning of the extraordinary arrangement of the basement in the keep at Flint? In all such donjons the cardinal defect was that once the enemy had broken in, the garrison were trapped. The

21 Farleigh Hungerford Castle

difficulty was sometimes met by providing a postern to enable them to escape. We must remember that the entrance was always the weak point. However carefully it might be secured, however stoutly defended, the assailants had more hope of battering it in than of breaching or mining the tower. Let us therefore imagine that an attacking party has forced the entrance to our donjon at Flint. Rushing along the narrow passage, in darkness and the confusion of assault, they stumble down a flight of steps into the comparatively small, well-like, vaulted and dimly lit chamber in the centre of the tower. But meantime the defenders have not been trapped. They escape round the gallery, and from its three doors they can sally forth upon the bewildered assailants. Clearly this is the purpose of the gallery. It is a kind of *place d'armes* affording access to three internal sally-ports, if I may use the term. For hand-to-hand fighting, it aimed to command the interior of the tower once this had been penetrated.[1]

Flint Castle has its immortal niche in history as the scene of the seizure, in defiance of a solemn oath, of Richard II—the first act in the Lancastrian usurpation which was to bring brief glory and ultimate prolonged disaster upon the realm and people of England. It was from the donjon of Flint Castle, where he had dined and heard mass in the chapel, that the hapless king descended into the courtyard on the afternoon of Tuesday, 22 August 1399, to meet his captor (and ultimately his murderer), Henry of Bolingbroke. Nothing can exceed the pathos of Froissart's contemporary narrative:

> King Richard had a greyhound called Matte, who always waited upon the King, and would know no man else. For whensoever the King did ride, he that kept the greyhound did let him loose, and he would straight run to the King and fawn upon him, and leap with his forefeet upon the King's shoulders. And as the King and Earl of Derby [Henry IV] talked together in the court, the greyhound who was wont to leap upon the King, left the King and came to the Earl of Derby, Duke of Lancaster, and made to him the same friendly countenance and cheer as he was wont to do to the King. The Duke, who knew not the greyhound,

---

[1] An alternative suggestion is that the mural gallery at Flint was designed as a bowman's gallery, like those at Caernarvon. But the Flint gallery has only three loopholes, and these at so low a level that they could cover only the waters of the moat. By contrast, the Caernarvon gallery loopholes are closely massed, and owing to the situation of the castle are able to command a good field.

demanded of the King what the greyhound would do. 'Cousin', quoth the King, 'it is a great good token to you, and an evil sign to me.' 'Sir, how know you that?' quoth the Duke. 'I know it well,' quoth the King. 'The greyhound maketh you cheer this day as King of England, as ye shall be and I shall be deposed; the greyhound has this knowledge naturally; therefore take him to you; he will follow you and forsake me.' The Duke understood well those words, and cherished the greyhound, who would never after follow King Richard, but followed the Duke of Lancaster.

The second castle built by Master James of St George for his royal client was at RHUDDLAN, a dozen miles, or thereby, further westward along the coast. Here we have a genuine concentric castle, but the keep-gatehouse conception has not been fully worked out. Rhuddlan is one of the most interesting historical sites in North Wales. Here the Welsh princes had a palace, which in 1063 was burned by Harold Godwinson, later the last Saxon King of England. His overthrow at Hastings in due course brought the Norman conquerors into Wales; and in 1073 a *motte* and bailey castle was thrown up at Rhuddlan by the deputy of the Norman Earl of Chester. The new owner, Robert of Rhuddlan, as he styled himself, also laid out, in dependence upon his castle, a regularly planned town, after the fashion already discussed in Chapter 5. The earthworks of the Norman castle and borough (which was important enough to possess its own mint) are still clearly visible to the east of the Edwardian settlement, which likewise consisted, as at Flint, of a strong stone castle to which was appended a borough enclosed by palisaded earthworks. The building records show that work upon the castle was begun on 14 September 1277, and was substantially completed by March 1282. From Rhuddlan, in 1284, King Edward issued his famous Statute of Wales—otherwise known as the Statute of Rhuddlan—a wise and generous enactment which gave the lands that his sword had won the constitution under which they were governed until the Tudor Act of Union in 1536. It is clear that at this time the King was planning to make Rhuddlan the capital of North Wales: indeed he negotiated with the Pope to transfer hither St Asaph's Cathedral. But the westward trend of conquest carried the King's plans along with it, and in the end it was Caernarvon that became the administrative and military capital of

Snowdonia. So Rhuddlan remains today as the memorial of an imperial project, abandoned almost as soon as conceived. This explains the extraordinary works which Edward carried out in connexion with his new castle and borough. To ensure safe access by sea, for purposes of

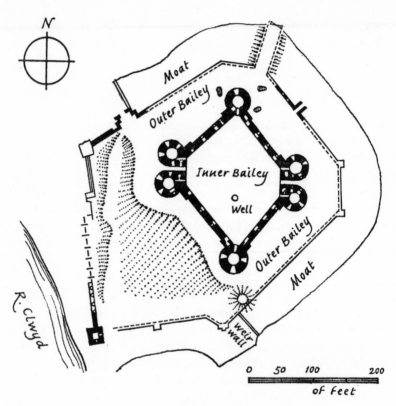

Plan of Rhuddlan Castle

war and peace, the channel of the River Clwyd was diverted and canalised, so that sea-going ships of large draft could come up to a quay beneath the castle. So enduring was Edward's achievement that Rhuddlan continued to be a port for coastwise shipping until so late as the advent of the railway. Direct access to the town from the hinterland was provided by a wooden bridge thrown across the new channel of the river, and so aligned as to bear directly upon the high street. The castle, further up the river, had its own quay, dockgate and rivergate, besides a gatehouse over against the new town, and another giving access to the former Norman borough.

The inner ward, or *Kernburg*, of Rhuddlan Castle forms a lozenge-shaped enclosure within lofty curtain walls, well loopholed for bow-shot defence. At two opposite angles are bold round towers: at the other two, paired towers enclose the two entrances. But these twin towers—'jemel towers', so they would have been called at the time of their building—are attached to no gatehouse, though there is documentary evidence of a timber rear-work. The outer ward is not strictly concentric, since it is extended down the riverside slope so as to control the quay. It is, however, well defended by loopholed curtains and square flanking towers. A remarkable feature about Rhuddlan Castle is the presence, if we include both wards, of no less than seven entrances. By the time that Conway and Caernarvon were built, the English conqueror had acquired a more wholesome respect for the 'wild Welsh'.

So thoroughly was Edward's work in Snowdonia done that, apart from the dramatic events connected with Richard II's dethronement, the subsequent history of Flint and Rhuddlan is comparatively quiet, until the Civil War, when both were held for the Crown, and, on capture, dismantled by order of Parliament. In 1652 Taylor the 'Water Poet' describes Rhuddlan as 'a wind and war shaken castle', and Flint (with some exaggeration) as 'almost buried in its own ruins'.

The building of Conway and Caernarvon followed, each with its borough attached: but in both the town defences now were towered walls of stone. Both castles were commenced in 1283, but whereas Conway was substantially finished by 1292, work at Caernarvon, owing to the financial difficulties of the King's later years, and the disastrous reign of his son, dragged on until 1323, and in the end the castle was left uncompleted. At Caernarvon, the master-mason James of St George was succeeded in turn by Master Walter of Hereford and Master Henry of Ellerton. These two castles rank among the grandest baronial ruins in Britain; and indeed Conway, castle and walled town, can have few rivals in western Europe. Owing to their rocky oblong sites, neither is a concentric castle. The unparalleled architectural magnificence of CAERNARVON CASTLE is certainly due to the fact that it was planned by King Edward I as a seat of the royal government, and the palace of the Prince of Wales; and that the plan, involving as it did the retention of a Norman *motte*, was designed to provide at Caernarvon the Windsor of Wales.[1] The foremost living authority on Edwardian castles has claimed Caernarvon as 'aesthetically perhaps the most satisfying secular building of its size which the Middle Ages have left to us'. Moreover, castle and town occupy a site famous in Welsh history and legend from Romano-Celtic times to the present day: so that, although an eighteenth-century Welsh topographer might describe it as 'that most magnificent badge of our subjection', to many it must seem, by contrast, that no

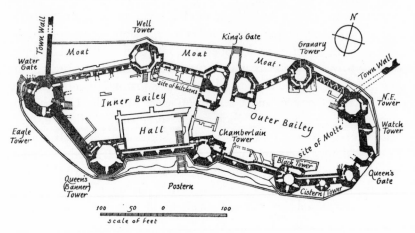

Plan of Caernarvon Castle

other place than *Y Gaer yn Arvon* provides 'a happier meeting-ground for vivid fantasy and romantic fact'. As a modern archaeologist has truly said, the locality is 'replete with the written and unwritten history of western Britain'.

Here, probably in the year A.D. 77 or 78, under the governorship of Julius Agricola, the Romans planted a cohort fort, to which, from the River Seiont whose estuary it overlooks, they gave the name Segontium. The final stage of this Roman post became inseparably associated, in the vivid memories of Dark Age Wales, with the remarkable figure of Magnus Maximus (A.D. 383–8). He is commonly classed among the long list of imperial usurpers, but this is only because he failed to do what his predecessor, Constantine the Great, another Emperor proclaimed by that turbulent army in Britain, successfully achieved.

[1] See my *Exploring Castles*, Chapters VII-IX.

Constantine was elevated by the garrison of York, and with that city his name is inseparably associated in later legend. It is therefore not improbable that Magnus Maximus received the imperial salutation, '*Maxime Auguste tu vincas*' at Segontium. This would account for the way in which 'Macsen Wledig', Prince Maxen, is associated with *Kaer Aber Sein* in later Welsh legend. It is averred that here at Caernarvon he married the Cornish Princess Helen, and that their son, Publicius, afterwards acquired sainthood. Under the Welsh form of his name, Pebly, he is commemorated at Llanbeblig, the mother-church of Caernarvon. Certainly Magnus Maximus was a most extraordinary man, whose career awaits study by a competent English scholar. In the circumstances, I may perhaps be excused for repeating what I have written about him in another context[1]:

> What lends a peculiar interest to the figure of Magnus Maximus in the eyes of the historical student is the fact that, unlike most of the military usurpers, he was no mere barrack-emperor, grounding his power on a mutinous army, but a man with a policy of his own, and a policy that shows him to have understood, like certain modern dictators, the art of harnessing on his own behalf some of the strongest impulses of his age.

Evan in our own prosaic day, the career and posthumous glory of this remarkable person has continued to attract romantic attention. He figures in the three most brilliant chapters of Kipling's *Puck of Pook's Hill*: and as 'Maxen Wledig' he is the hero of the only published portion of Katherine Buck's monumental *Wayland-Dietrich Saga*. How much of all this rainbow glory of a Celtic past was present in the mind of Edward Plantagenet when he finally chose Caernarvon as the capital of a revived Principality of Wales? And what legendary memories of Maxen Wledig's glittering palace were behind his decision to create, here on the ancient site, the most resplendent of English Castles?

The plan of Caernarvon Castle may be approximately described as an irregular oblong with a narrow waist, across which a transverse building, conceived as an integral part of the fortification, divides the interior enclosure into an upper or eastern and a lower or western ward. Around the cincture of curtain walling by which both these wards are fenced is set a majestic array of multangular towers, thirteen in all, including the double-towers of the two gatehouses, both opening into

[1] *St Ninian and the Origins of the Christian Church in Scotland*, p. 56.

the upper ward: the King's Gate facing northwards towards the town, and the Queen's Gate at the extreme eastern apex of the castle. Largest of all is the Eagle Tower at the opposite end, which retains something of the special character of the now old-fashioned donjons. But the most remarkable structure in the castle is the King's Gate. It appears never to have been finished; but enough evidence survives to show that a formidably defended entrance, equipped with no less than five pairs of folding doors and six portcullises, not to speak of 'murder-holes' in the vaulted passage, led through to a central multangular gate-hall, from which transverse passages, similarly secured, led right and left respectively to the lower and the upper wards. The Queen's Gate is smaller and of simpler design. There are also a postern in the Eagle Tower, another in the Well Tower, and a third from the great hall. Little but foundations now survive of the interior buildings, which included a large hall in the lower ward. Most unusually, there is no castle chapel, but at least five oratories were provided in various towers. But it is impossible here to give any idea of the complicated defensive arrangements of this astonishing castle. Indeed they can be fully realised only by a visit (and that not a brief one) to the castle. But mention must be made of the mural galleries, sometimes at two levels, by which the lofty and massive curtain walls are threaded. Along these galleries easy access was obtained from tower to tower; moreover, they are furnished with numerous bowslits, many of which are arranged in groups of three, converging upon one external loophole, so that each could be served by three archers, shooting in turn. Above all was the embrasured parapet. Such a triple line of defence, manned by the foremost bowmen in Western Europe, affords to this day a silent witness of the wholesome respect in which the Welsh were held by the English garrison of Caernarvon.

A remarkable feature of this castle is the lofty and slender octagonal turrets which rise above the massive towers. The Eagle Tower has no less than three of these, and as they are expanded upwards by successive string courses, the effect is somewhat ungainly. Indeed the whole aspect of Caernarvon Castle represents something completely novel in English castellar construction. This is due not only to the multangular form adopted in the towers, but also to the banded masonry, formed by the insertion, at intervals amid the light coloured limestone ashlar, of brown sandstone courses. Here we must recognise the personal taste of

22 *Bolton Castle from the west*
23 *Rhuddlan Castle from the north west*

Master James of St George: for in his native Savoy he built multangular towers at the Castle of St Georges d'Espérance—the town from which doubtless the great architect derived his name; and in the neighbour-hood is another large, octagonal tower with banded masonry, perhaps likewise the work of Master James. The Theodosian walls of Constan-tinople have likewise banded masonry and octagonal towers; and I have little doubt that James of St George had seen them.

The upper ward of Caernarvon Castle is bulged out all round on plan so as to enclose the Norman *motte*, the last remnants of which survived until as late as 1870. Had he so wished, it would have been perfectly easy for Edward I to remove this earthwork. That it was deliberately left is shown not only by the way in which the Edwardian curtains and towers are carried round it, but also because here, and here alone, the curtains are provided with a broad massive apron or retaining plinth. We can hardly conceive that this revetment was designed to resist an outward thrust of the *motte*, which must long since have settled down firmly upon its rocky stance. Evidently it was intended to rear upon the *motte* a lofty tower, dominating the entire castle, like Edward III's remodelling of the round tower that crowns the *motte* at Windsor. Plantagenet imperialism was to have a second capital in the new Principality of Wales.

So thoroughly was Edward's work in Snowdonia done that the history of Caernarvon Castle in the later medieval period is comparatively uneventful. In 1403 it was unsuccessfully besieged by Owain Glyndwr, aided by a French contingent. With the complete embodiment of Wales into the English political system by the Act of Union in 1536, Caernarvon lost most of its military and administrative importance, and the castle in consequence fell rapidly into decay. During the Civil War town and castle sustained three sieges in the cause of Charles I; but the castle appears to have suffered little or not at all. Its moment of extreme danger came after the Restoration, when the government, in agreement with the county and borough councils, decided that the castle and town walls should be demolished 'for the advantage of our-selves and posterity' (!)—the expense to be met by the sale of their timber, lead and stone. Fortunately this proposal came to nothing.

24 Harlech Castle

Doubtless it was found that the profit would not match the cost. Caernarvon Castle has never ceased to be crown property, and is now maintained as a national monument. In the long line of its constables the most famous name is that of David Lloyd George, a statue of whom stands before the Queen's Gate—though his figure seems oddly insignificant in front of the majestic work of Edward Plantagenet.

In the last two castles erected by Edward I to secure his hold on North Wales, James of St George reverted to, and achieved his masterpieces in, his favourite concentric plan. The Castle of Harlech on the Monmouth-shire coast was erected between 27 May 1285 and 27 December 1291, at a total cost of £8598 6s 9d—a sum equal probably to something like £1,000,000 at the present day. By contrast with the rapid completion of Harlech, Beaumaris Castle on the Anglesey side of the Menai Strait, begun in 1295, was in the end left incomplete in 1321. Of both these splendid buildings I have written elsewhere. Suffice it here to say about Harlech Castle that it represents the concentric plan, combined with a keep-gatehouse, in its most logical form. Every component part is fully developed, and nothing is superfluous or non-essential. In the anatomy of its construction, simplicity and directness of design are the keynotes, and the castle, at first sight stern and repelling on its proud rocky stance, reveals on analysis the full austere beauty of expressive structure. Beaumaris Castle has always attracted attention through the remarkable symmetry of its design: a quadrangular inner ward, with round towers at the four corners and midway on each flank; (very remarkably) two keep-gatehouses, in front and rear; and a low mult-angular outer wall, garnished with no less than twelve small towers, two minor gatehouses and a spur-walk guarding the dock. With a compass at the centre, you may draw a series of circles, each linking up the different towers and angles in their several positions. In a former study of Beaumaris Castle, I put forward the view that the provision of a second keep-gatehouse was a breach of structural verity, due to the pushing of the quest for symmetry in defiance of practical requirements. Further reflection has led me to the conclusion that so great an architect as James of St George would be the last person to provide his castle with a superfluity—particularly in view of the

straitened finances of his royal client. I now unreservedly accept the
contrary view expressed by Mr Arnold Taylor in the following terms:[1]

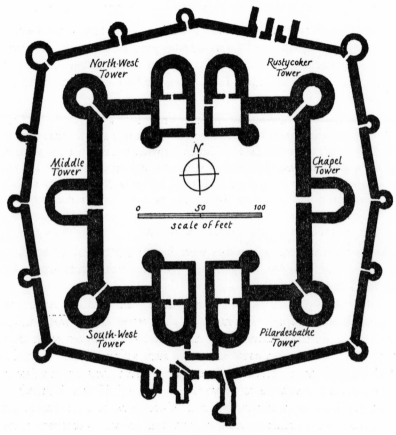

Plan of Beaumaris Castle

Dr Simpson argues that the presence of two keep-gatehouses at Beaumaris, as compared with the one at Harlech, is a source of weakness
rather than of strength. When, however, one considers the essential
difference between the two sites, the one a steep rocky promontory above
the coast, the other at sea-level and practically on the beach, the design
appears to rest on sound principles in each case. At Harlech an attack
in strength could come only from the land; there is therefore a single

[1] *English Hist. Review*, vol. LXV, p. 448, n.4.

keep-gatehouse facing the land. At Beaumaris attack might well come either along the shore or from the landward side, or from both directions at once; provision is accordingly made to meet the double risk by building two keep-gatehouses, one facing inland and one towards the beach.

Anyhow, both pairs of gatehouse towers at Beaumaris were deemed worthy of being equipped for mounting guns so late as 1558, when, during the inglorious war with France that cost England the loss of Calais, her last foothold upon French soil, the Earl of Bath wrote to the Privy Council

> beseeching your lordships further that I may have a warrant to Sir John Salisbury, the Queen's Majesty's receiver in those parts, to cause reparations to be done upon the four principal towers within the inner ward of the said castle, which be the place where the ordinance have been laid on, for the better defence of the said castle, and now they be ruins as they cannot be placed there, and that he may have a commission also to take timber for these reparations, out of the woods of the Abbey of Conway; otherwise there is no timber within the isle that will serve this purpose.

Obviously both keep-gatehouses were being refurbished for artillery, a fact that confirms Mr Taylor's view that they were equivalent in the castle scheme.

Nine castles of the first rank were built by Edward I to secure the English hold of Wales. Insomuch as they were royal undertakings, intended to subserve national ends, they are State fortresses rather than feudal castles in the ordinary sense. No such building effort in public defence was seen in Britain between the Roman forts on the Saxon Shore and the coastal defence works of Henry VIII and Elizabeth I. Since the Edwardian castles in North Wales were paid for out of the royal purse, the building accounts have been in part preserved in the public accounts. I have already given the total bill for the case of Harlech. The extraordinary organisational effort thus involved has been the subject of much detailed study in recent years. Suffice it here to say that at Beaumaris alone in 1296 Master James of St George was directing the operations of 400 masons, 2000 labourers, 200 quarrymen, 30 smiths and carpenters, 100 carts, 60 wagons, and 30 cargo boats. And all this for one castle only! What tremendous effort was involved in the accumulation of men and beasts, materials and supplies, in remote, inaccessible and dangerous localities; the formidable problems of transport; the organisation and feeding of the labour forces; the protection of the working parties; the detailed and accurate accounting. English, Scots and Welsh will never agree in their verdict upon Edward I. Even his staunchest admirers must admit that he was guilty of many deeds of violence and cruelty in pursuit of his grand ideal of the unity of Britain. His defenders have sometimes claimed that he is entitled to be judged according to the standard of his times. Yet any such apology may well seem gratuitous in our terrible twentieth century, in which rulers and states have perpetrated deeds of mass cruelty upon a scale which would have left the worst medieval tyrant speechless with horror. With all such arguments we are not here concerned. What stands forth luminously from the record is the great king's extraordinary force of will and tenacity of purpose, his military genius and administrative capacity, his firm conviction that conquest must be followed by legislative settlement, and his ability to find and to use, in all his varied undertakings, men of the calibre of Master James of St George.

But the record of military building in Wales during the Edwardian Conquest is not closed with the nine royal castles. The marcher-barons were active on their own, and in at least one case the King is known to have helped with money and the loan of royal masons. In 1282 Henry de Lacy, Earl of Lincoln and Salisbury, and a close confidant of the King, received a grant of the lordship of Denbigh in Flintshire, in order that he might there establish a castellated borough of the approved Edwardian pattern. Building was started immediately, and before the end of the year six royal masons were employed upon the job. The town walls, which include a segment of the castle *enceinte*, are built after the common form, with round towers like those of the town defences at Conway and Caernarvon. But on the townward front of the castle we meet with the unmistakable handiwork of Master James of St George: banded masonry, multangular towers, and a remarkable triangular gatehouse, consisting of three towers, two in front covering the portal, and a third in rear, with a central multangular gatehall and an L-shaped passage giving access to the courtyard. The resemblance between this Denbigh gatehouse and the uncompleted King's Gate at Caernarvon is obvious at a glance.

Saving only the Tower of London, the most remarkable concentric castle in Britain is CAERPHILLY in Glamorgan, about seven miles north of Cardiff. This also, like Denbigh, was the work of a subject: Gilbert de Clare, ninth Earl of Gloucester, Earl of Hertford, and son-in-law of Edward I. It took a long time to build; and in its final form, including the water defences, the castle covers an area of no less than thirty acres.

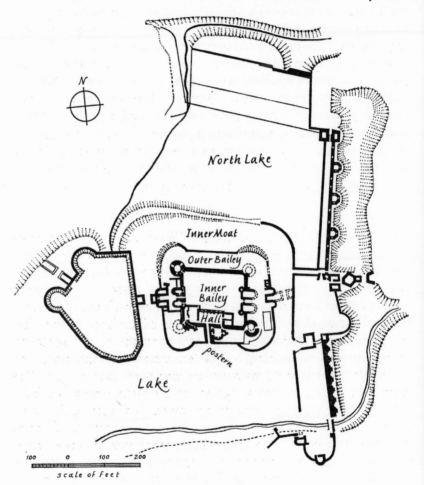

Plan of Caerphilly Castle

The central portion is a typical concentric castle with outer and inner wards, and having two keep-gatehouses, like Beaumaris. On the western side there is a third large bastioned enclosure or hornwork, quite separate from the main castle; and the *enceinte* was completed on the east side by a most astonishing fortified barrage, about 380 yards in length, with a heavily defended gatehouse, spanning the valley in which the castle is built, and damming its two streams so as to form a lake about 12 feet deep, large enough to enclose the whole castle, including the hornwork, from which the main structure is isolated by a cross-arm of the lake. This dam, with its massive buttresses to resist the pressure of the water, reminds us of the barrages which the Hydro-electric Boards have built in so many of our upland valleys.

Up till recently, students of this tremendous castle have tended to believe that the whole immense fabric was substantially the work of one continuous and rapid effort of building upon a preconceived plan. But in 1937 a different view was propounded by the late Professor William Rees:

> We cannot exclude the possibility that the castle, as originally designed, consisted only of the citadel, the main gateway of which was on the west side and covered by the hornwork. In that case the outer curtain, with the water defences, was the work of slightly later date, when the full possibilities of the site had become apparent.

A careful study of the structure suggests that in the theory thus tentatively put forward by Rees lies the key to the evolution of this noble castle. It seems clear that its development was a good deal more complicated than has often been supposed and that the work of building continued over an extended period, during which radical alterations and additions were made to the original design.

In the first place, it should be noted that the eastern gatehouse of the main castle is both larger and more elaborate than the western one. The western gatehouse indeed is an ordinary fortified entry of the traditional thirteenth-century type, having the principal apartment on the first floor. By contrast, the eastern gatehouse is an Edwardian keep-gatehouse, with the peculiarity, characteristic of such structures, of relegating the castellan's hall to the second floor, the first floor forming a fighting deck. It has the usual frontal portcullis, behind which are folding doors: there are also rearward doors, closing against the court-yard. On the other hand the western gatehouse had an outer gate only, closing against the exterior, with a portcullis outside: there is also an inner portcullis, but no rearward gate. On this assumption, the castle was later turned about, and the eastern gatehouse constructed, with the powerful outworks retaining the lake.[1] At present, the bank dividing the inner moat from the northern lake seems superfluous. Sir Charles Oman dismissed it as 'a spit of gravel' devoid of 'tactical meaning', a mere 'accident of terrain which the builder of the castle did not think it worth while to dig away'. But this bank is certainly more than an accident of terrain or a spit of gravel. It is a regular earthwork, and obviously is the counterscarp of the moat whose waters it served to retain. It can best be explained on the assumption that the northern lake at first was not there.

If the above reading be true, the original castle of Caerphilly will have closely resembled Harlech, having a double envelope; single gatehouse, facing west, upon the inner ward; outer or barbican gatehouse corresponding thereto; moat or ditch enclosing all, save on the southern side where the marshes along the Nant-y-Gledyr rendered this unnecessary (as the rock did at Harlech). What then about the so-called hornwork? On the basis of the view above set forth as to the evolution of Caerphilly Castle, this earthwork falls into its natural position as a basecourt in front of the original castle. We have seen that at Flint, main castle, basecourt, and fenced town form an articulated whole—the first of the colonial towns, on the model of a French *bastide*, which Edward I built to police and civilise his newly-won territories in North Wales. I suspect that a similar conception underlay the primary deployment at Caerphilly: that it was proposed at the outset to attach a *bastide* to the Castle, and that the whole scheme was a deliberate attempt to introduce 'civility', as the Anglo-Normans understood it, among the 'wild Welsh' of upper Glamorgan. On this assumption, the site originally proposed for the borough of Caerphilly will have been to the north-west of the castle. With its good drainage and sunward exposure, this site is a better position than the lower one now occupied by the town. The old paved road leading out from the 'hornwork' to the higher ground on the north-west certainly seems to suggest that the borough was at first intended to be sited here. It is perhaps not without significance that an early nineteenth-century topographer says that here was a piece of ground called 'Burgesses Field'.

---

[1] For a similar case of a castle that seems to have been turned around about, see my paper, 'The Development of Helmsley Castle', in *The Fourth Viking Congress*, ed. A. Small, pp. 166–75.

25 Harlech Castle

As a triumph of hydraulic engineering, the great barrage at Caerphilly deserves respectful study by the modern practitioners of that austere calling. The northern half of the dam, beyond the gatehouse, is in effect a double wall, strengthened and defended by three rectangular towers. The southern half is expanded into a broad earthen platform, revetted in rear, and in front retained by a wall no less than 15 feet thick, and further strengthened by ten massive buttresses. Between these buttresses, the wall faces are built with a ramping concavity, so as to form a series, as it were, of vaults up-ended. These vaults and the buttresses, with the great thickness of the wall and the massive bank behind, are clearly designed to resist an enormous pressure from the west. Obviously the engineer had in mind the winter floods of the Nant-y-Gledyr. So far as I know, this construction with what may be called vertical vaults is unique in medieval work; but it is found in sixteenth-century curtains designed to withstand a cannonade. The buttresses are large enough to carry defensive platforms, so that the southern section of the barrage, despite its length of 290 feet or thereby, is as adequately flanked as is the northern.

Earl Gilbert de Clare is stated to have begun the building of Caerphilly Castle on 11 April 1268. Two years later the building, to whatever state it had reached, was seized and burnt by Llywelyn ap Gruffydd. In the great Welsh revolt of 1294, the town of Caerphilly was given to the flames, but the castle held out. In 1314, after the young Earl of Gloucester had fallen at Bannockburn, the Welsh of Glamorgan rose again and attacked the castle, but failed to penetrate it, though the 'outward defences', presumably still of timber, were reduced to ashes. By marrying a Clare heiress, Edward II's favourite, Hugh le Despenser the younger, obtained possession of the lordship of Glamorgan, and with it the Castle of Caerphilly. Here, therefore, on the invasion of England by his exiled Queen, Isabella 'the She-wolf of France' and her paramour Roger Mortimer, the hapless King Edward II, after wandering about in South Wales, obtained brief shelter. After his capture the castle still held out, but on 20 March 1327 it surrendered, and all the King's personal belongings, plate, jewellery and money fell into the vengeful Queen's hands. Hugh le Despenser is known to have been building at Caerphilly in 1326, upon a scale that demanded the employment of a master mason and a master carpenter of the first rank. The later history of the castle is comparatively uneventful. By Tudor times

26   *Caernarvon Castle*
27   *Yanwath Hall, south front*

it was far gone in decay. Though record appears to be silent as to its fortunes in the Civil War, the castle has plainly been blown up; and the bastioned earthwork to the north-west has very much the appearance of a redoubt dating from that period. In the nineteenth century Caerphilly was inherited by the noble house of Bute, and by the third Marquis the immense task was taken in hand of repairing the huge pile of ruins, and clearing away the shabby old houses by which the site was encumbered. This work, which went far beyond mere con-solidation, but involved much scholarly restoration, was continued by his successor. One portion, however, has been left unrestored: the famous 'Leaning Tower', the surviving fragment of which has been blown off the plumb by the explosion which destroyed the tower. In 1950 Lord Bute handed over the castle to the custody of the Ministry of Works. Since then the repairs have been continued, and the waters of the lake, which had been drained by breaching the barrage when the castle was dismantled, have been restored—the northern sector indeed had been flooded by Lord Bute. The effect is magnificent. Quite unexpectedly, in exploring the Civil War redoubt, the remains of a first-century Roman fort have been revealed.

It should not be thought that the Edwardian keep-gate houses are confined to concentric castles. At Tonbridge in Kent, another castle of the de Clares, we find a large keep-gatehouse, most formidably secured, added to a mount-and-bailey castle. Here the self-contained jealousy of the keep-gatehouse is carried to a climax. The entrance, as usual, is guarded by portcullises in front and rear, by two pairs of folding gates (the inner pair closing against the courtyard), and by 'murder-holes' in the vaulted passage. Not only this, but even the side doors into the lodges, and the doors leading out on to the wall-walks, are all port-cullised. At Llanstephan in Carmarthen and Dunstanburgh in North-umberland are massive keep-gatehouses in castles that were never concentric. The last two examples illustrate a defect which beset the keep-gatehouse theme, and resulted in its abandonment before the fourteenth century was out. This defect arose from the attempt to combine a lord's residence with a gatehouse. We can readily understand how the interpolation of the drawbridge and portcullis machinery, into the midst of what should have been the principal residential apartments of the castellan, must have been awkward in more than one respect. At Caernarvon, Harlech and elsewhere, the portcullis is actually operated from the chapel—surely a case, if ever, of the church militant! At Dunstanburgh, Llanstephan and Tonbridge, the difficulty was got over by relegating the great hall to the second floor; but from a domestic viewpoint such an arrangement was obviously inconvenient. So at Llanstephan and Dunstanburgh the keep-gatehouse was soon given up as a house of entry. Its passage was built up, and a new entrance made in the curtain wall on the flank. There are other examples of the same alteration, both in Scotland and in Ireland. The whole phenomenon of these keep-gatehouses, and the way in which the scheme had often to be abandoned before a long time had elapsed, must therefore be regarded as a product of the tensions set up by the tug-of-war between comfort and defence which lies at the root of the development of castellar design in the later Middle Ages.

8

The Northern Tower-houses

HAUGHTON CASTLE in Northumberland occupies a situation of striking beauty on the right bank of the North Tyne, about two miles above the picturesque village of Hunshaugh. It stands with its back to the crest of a steep bank overhanging the riverside haugh from which presumably the place is called. Successively the seat of the Pratt, Swinburn and Widdrington families, the castle, doubtless because it was a place of minor importance, does not bulk large in the annals of the Scottish wars of the fourteenth and fifteenth centuries. But in 1541, being then in a neglected condition, it was raided by the Armstrongs, Elliots, and other Border clans; a second raid followed in 1587. Latterly the castle has been a seat of the Cruddas family, by whom it has been carefully restored.

On approaching Haughton, we at once gain the impression of something quite unusual among English castles. This is due to the great length, height, and narrowness of the building, with its square corner turrets, themselves embattled, rising above the embattled wall-heads. Along the side walls will be seen an arcade of five broad pointed arches, resting upon buttresses; and the whole building has also been heightened. A mid-thirteenth-century date is clearly indicated by the architectural detail of the primary work. Careful inspection of the interior reveals that the five large arches on either side each screened a long machicolation. We have therefore in this castle probably the earliest British example of what may be termed 'buttress-machicolations'. This device originated in the fortified churches of the twelfth and thirteenth centuries in Provence. It was adapted by Richard Coeur-de-Lion for his great donjon of Château Gaillard. In the fourteenth century the device became common, and finds its most majestic expression in the Papal

Palace at Avignon. So far as I am aware, the only other example in England is found, as a fourteenth-century addition, on the west side of the town walls at Southampton. Probably this formidable defensive arrangement in the thirteenth-century hall-house of Haughton should be construed as a product of tension between Henry III and Alexander III of Scotland, which in 1244 and 1258 brought the two kingdoms to the brink of war.

Haughton Castle, then, is a strongly fortified hall-house. It is important to remember that such a hall-house represents the normal medieval scheme. To us it seems exceptional merely because, being in most cases of timber, it has so rarely survived. By contrast the rectangular stone tower-house, which in northern England seems so typical of a smaller medieval baron's dwelling, really represents an abnormal development, due to the militarisation of society in the Scottish wars. The tower-house, typically containing cellarage in its basement, hall on the first floor, and solar above that, is simply the hall-house plan upended for security reasons. Nothing could be more perverse than J. A. Gotch's contention that 'the first germ of the house of today is to be found in the Norman Keep'. The truth is just the other way round. The house of today is derived from the medieval hall-house. The keep or tower-house represents an exceptional and aberrant development, due to a compulsive quest for safety.

In their various forms, these rectangular tower-houses form a characteristic and striking feature in the Border landscape. One of the best known, which I have described elsewhere,[1] is the Vicar's Pele at Corbridge—the fortified residence of the parish priest. To such a tower-house the word 'pele' or peel is applied as a transferred epithet. Derived from late Latin *palus*, a stake, it properly belongs to the palisade by which these tower-houses were often surrounded. There is a very similar 'vicar's pele' at Embleton, near Dunstanburgh Castle on the Northumbrian coast.

Though no two of them are precisely alike, inevitably these northern tower-houses are 'much of a muchness'. We shall therefore content ourselves with describing two examples, one of which, however, is perhaps the most impressive of them all. BELSAY CASTLE, in the parish of Bolam, Northumberland, stands on the western side of the Newcastle-Jedburgh road, about fifteen miles north-west from Newcastle. In

[1] *Exploring Castles*, p. 103.

medieval times the road from Newcastle, *via* Otterburn to Jedburgh
and Teviotdale, was of prime importance as a line of communication
between England and Scotland. Hence Belsay Castle occupied a position
of no little strategic consequence. From at least the early thirteenth
century, with one lapse due to forfeiture in 1318, there have been
Middletons in Belsay; and under Henry III their representative, Richard
de Middleton, was successively Keeper of the Great Seal and Chancellor
of England. A manor house existed before the present castle, and in
December 1278 was visited for several days by Edward I. After the forfeiture the manor passed in 1335 to Sir John de Strivelyn (or Stirling),
a distinguished soldier in the Edward III's wars. He was a relative of
the Middletons, and so Belsay in due course reverted to the old family.
The date of erection of the tower-house is not on record, but its is clear
from the architectural evidence that it must have been a-building during
the time when the manor was alienated; and surely it is significant that
the place was then in the hands of a distinguished soldier, who was
responsible for important works undertaken by the English during their
occupation of Edinburgh Castle in 1336. The record reveals him as the
lord of many manors and valuable perquisites, both in his own right
and in those of his two wives; the recipient, moreover, of munificent
gifts from the sovereign whom he had served so well, alike in the
cabinet and in the field. Clearly he was a man of wealth and taste, fully
able to build himself so large, well-designed and ornate a tower-house,
even in the war-blasted county of Northumberland.

Every piece of sound architecture responds to the spirit of its time.
The keynote of the fourteenth century was its superficial and flaunting
brilliance. This was the age when formal chivalry and knight-errantry,
with their love of pageantry and their insistence upon the external
graces of high life—valour and courtesy—reached their most fantastic
development. Thus we find Philip of France and Edward of England
planning to decide the issue of a great international quarrel in single
combat, man to man. Again, the Black Prince waits in person at the
table of his royal captive, King John of France; or, yet again, a lady's
hand is staked to the gallant knight who shall hold the Castle Dangerous
for a year and a day against the craft and skill in arms of the redoubtable
'Black Douglas'. The best picture of the formal and extravagant chivalry
which characterised this age will be found in the vivid pages of
Froissart. And nowhere does this flamboyant phase of late medieval

civilisation express itself with greater dazzle than in the England of Edward III. At home, the inefficient rule of his hapless father gave place to a strong and generally wise administration, which guaranteed internal peace and security from foreign aggression. Abroad, English armies and fleets achieved victories that made the name of England resound through the western world. Despite the Black Death, the material prosperity of the country increased by leaps and bounds, and the middle classes especially made great strides towards a higher standard of well-being. The Commons gradually achieved and consolidated a large measure of political authority, without recourse to internal strife such as had distracted the preceding era. If the Church was passing into its decline it was still a potent and resplendent organisation, whose magnificent shrines and stately ritual exerted an enormous influence for good. Lastly, the complete blending of Saxon, Dane and Norman into an English nation was marked by the emergence of a noble vernacular literature in which, as John Richard Green has finely said, we discern 'the new gladness of a great people'.

As in other things, so in architecture. The flamboyant exuberance of the English spirit in the great days of Edward of Windsor formed its expression in the Decorated phase of Gothic building—the most brilliant and romantic development in the whole range of medieval architecture. Among secular buildings, no better illustration of this 'arrogant splendour'—to borrow John Warrack's phrase—can be found than Belsay Castle. It is the embodiment, in stone and lime, of the fantastic chivalry, the uninhibited gaiety, of the third Edward's court. In its own medium it expresses the same mood as the extravagant peacetime costume, and the bizarre panoply on the field of war, with which the gallant band of warriors whom the brilliant king drew together at his Table Round, adorned their dignity of rank and set forth their pride of prowess. The very spirit of that far-off time seems to be portrayed in the martial yet fantastic profile of the Belsay tower-house. Looking at its rumbustious skyline, I am irresistibly reminded of Blind Harry's description of the contemporary Yorkshire castle of Ravensworth:

A royal stead, fast by a forest side,
With turrets fair, and garrets of great pride,
Builded about, right likely to be wight.
Awful it was unto any man's sight.

Externally, Belsay Castle appears to be an almost square tower-house, with a shallow recess in the middle of the western face. But this outside aspect obscures the real design of the castle, which consists of a rectangular tower, with its axis north and south, and having on the west side two projecting wings, which between them enclose the entrance passage, the door being covered by a *bretasche* opening from the second floor. The main building contains three lofty rooms, one above the other. The lowest, which is vaulted and contains the castle well, was at first a store, later converted into a kitchen, with a large fireplace inserted in its north wall. The rooms above formed respectively the hall and upper hall or solar. In the southern wing is the spiral stair, circling up to the summit of the tower, and also a series of six small rooms, of which the two lowest and the two topmost rooms are vaulted. That on the hall level formed the original 'kitchenette', as in the very similar tower-house at Chapchase Castle. It has a service hatch to the stair, and doubtless had a fireplace in the position now occupied by an inserted window. In the other wing are four storeys of apartments —a vaulted cellar, reached by a passage from the entrance lobby, and three large, unvaulted living rooms above. Stout yet comely corbelled turrets, each containing a vaulted chamber, crown three angles of the tower; and the stair-head, with its associated rooms, forms a fourth turret, larger and loftier than the others. Round the main building runs a boldly corbelled and machicolated parapet, and similar but smaller parapets crown the turrets. Important remains of medieval wall-painting in the great hall add to the charm and interest of this fascinating tower. A change in the character of the ashlar masonry, and a different suite of mason's marks, point to a pause in the building—perhaps due to the Black Death in 1348.

Few English castles are more fortunate in their setting than Belsay. The house which its owners tacked on to their ancient tower in 1614 is as charming a little piece of Renaissance design as anything in Northumberland; and, now that a lumbering eighteenth-century addition has been removed, Plantagenet tower and Jacobean hall are mated in a seemly partnership in which neither loses its identity while each seems perfectly matched with the other. And the immense Doric mansion which in 1810 Sir Charles Monck, a Middleton who changed his name in deference to a lucrative bequest, built hard by the ancient castle, is a *tour de force* of the highest architectural merit. It has been combined with

a landscape setting, deliberately designed to enhance it, in a manner which makes this whole group of Belsay Castle, old and new, with its attendant lay-out of gardens and grounds, and the planned village outside the demesne, one of the most interesting manorial *ensembles* to be found anywhere in England.

Our second example of a northern Border tower-house is YANWATH HALL, in Westmorland, on a bold wooded bluff overlooking the bonny Vale of Eamont, about two miles south of Penrith. The tower, to which a hall and later buildings have been added, is believed to have been built by one of the Threlkeld family early in the fourteenth century. It commands an important ford over the Eamont, from which it is about half a bowshot distant. The tower contains three storeys; a vaulted cellar, a first-floor hall, and an upper hall or solar. At the north end of the east door is the pointed arched door, on the right hand side of which opens a spiral stair, steep and narrow as the way of righteousness. This stair serves both upper floors, and reaches the flat leaded roof which forms the fighting deck of the tower. The hall is now lit by three Tudor windows, and is covered with a fine wooden ceiling, on which was formerly visible the date 1586. The solar has an open timber roof and windows with side benches. Both rooms are well fitted up with fireplaces, wall-presses and privies. A simple moulded cornice carries the battlements, and at all four corners are square turrets, battlemented similarly to the main tower. These turrets contain small chambers beneath flat stone platforms reached from the leads by external stairs of stone. One finely moulded octagonal chimney stack, with an open cowl, still remains. It is of good fourteenth century pattern, and strongly resembles the well-known one at Grosmont Castle, Monmouthshire.

Towards the end of the fourteenth century a hall-block was added on the eastern side of the tower-house. The original purpose of such a hall was to accommodate the retainers at a common board, leaving the tower for the exclusive use of the lord and his family. The hall-block was much pulled about in the fifteenth and sixteenth centuries, but the original arrangements have not been radically disturbed. The dais was at the west end, next the tower, and was distinguished by a tall and very beautiful oriel window of three trifoliated and transomed lights. The body of the hall is lit by a couple of shorter windows, each of two trefoiled lights. At the lower end of the hall is a stone screen of the sixteenth century, evidently replacing a medieval predecessor. The servery behind has doors at either end, a fashion persisting in Elizabethan houses. Above an inserted plaster ceiling the hall retains a fine open-timbered roof of the fifteenth century. Beyond the servery is the kitchen, which was almost entirely reconstructed in Tudor times. Then or subsequently, ranges were added to enclose a courtyard behind the tower and hall-house. The whole group of buildings includes many features of interest, in which the delight in grace of form and vigour in execution which the old craftsmen brought to their labour is abundantly manifest.

Yanwath, observed Thomas Marshall, the seventeenth-century historian of Westmorland, 'hath a delicate prospect when you are at it, and hath the grace of a little castle when you depart from it'. Although nowadays the west-coast expresses thunder past within a stone's cast of its wall, this fine example of a small Border stronghold retains a full measure of its ancient grace, while the 'delicate prospect' from its time-worn battlements is little impaired by all the changes that have taken place since Marshall wrote. The view from the tower-head is indeed a splendid one. On the west are the Cumbrian fells, with Helvellyn and Saddleback in all their glory. Eastward, the broad strath of the Eden valley is generously displayed, with the fine outline of the Pennines beyond. To the south extends an ample rolling champaign country: and immediately under the castle to the north lies the romantic deep and wooded valley of the Eamont, with Penrith Beacon in the middle distance beyond.[1]

It is important to remember that these northern tower-houses are not the great crown fortresses or the strongholds of capital lords. They are the residences of the intermediate and smaller landowners; and the point about them is that they are entirely different from the sort of dwelling in which these people had been living before the disastrous attack upon Scotland. Previous to that unhappy venture, the country squires had lived in timber or stone-built halls. We can study at Aydon

[1] For Yanwath see my paper in *Trans. C. & W. Society*, n.s., vol. XLIV (1945), pp. 55–67, where I have shown that the Royal Commission on Historical Monuments were mistaken in considering the tower-house and hall-house to be contemporary. It is right to say that the late Sir Alfred Clapham, Secretary of the Commission, informed me (in a letter dated 15 September 1945) that difficulties were placed in the way of the Commission's officers in making their survey. My own study was made under much more favourable circumstances.

Castle, near Corbridge, how such a peaceful establishment, in those iron years of war, had to be enclosed by a fortified wall; and we have its builder's own word for it, in 1315, that 'he had lately fortified his dwelling house at Aydon with a wall of stone and lime against the King's enemies, the Scots'. Where a house was being erected *de novo*, it had perforce, under the new conditions, to be designed as a strong fortalice. For such requirements, in the case of a landowner of moderate resources, the scheme of a simple rectangular tower was obviously the most defensible and the most convenient. In all ages and in all countries, the simplest way to achieve security has been to live in a tower: 'Be unto us, O Lord, a strong tower; from the face of our enemies'.

In the present chapter and its two predecessors, we have seen that, as a general rule, the donjon or tower-house, whether rectangular or circular, passed out of the realm of current English castellar construction in the course of the fourteenth century, except in the war-torn northern shires. Nevertheless, even in the more settled south and east, we find that one or two rectangular tower-houses were erected in the fourteenth century. One of these, Longthorpe Tower near Peterborough, with its wonderful mural paintings, I have discussed in another work.[1] More remarkable, at least architecturally, is NUNNEY CASTLE in Somerset, about three and a half miles south-west of the pleasant market town of Frome, in a green and sheltered vale overlooked by the eastern spur of the Mendips. On 28 November 1373 Sir John de la Mare, whose family had owned the manor at least since 1256, received the royal licence 'to fortify and crenellate his manse at Nunney in the county of Somerset with a wall of stone and lime'. It was evidently then that the fine tower-house, which alone of the buildings now survives, was erected. Collinson in his *History of Somerset* (1791), says that Sir John embellished the castle 'with spoils brought from abroad which had been won in the wars of France'. Nunney must therefore rank with Bodiam and Shirburn and Bolton as one of a group of castles built by veterans of the Edward III's campaigns, and in their robust martial character reflecting something of the militaristic outlook of their builders—all of them professional soldiers of the new type that the Hundred Years' War was breeding.

---

[1] *Exploring Castles*, pp. 98–100.

Moreover, Nunney, like Bodiam and Farleigh Hungerford—though the builder of the latter was a civilian rather than a warrior—was erected at a period when, as we saw (p. 95), all the southern parts of England were in dread of a French invasion. In September 1645 the owner, Colonel Richard Prater, stood a two days' siege on behalf of Charles I. After its fall, the castle as usual was condemned to be 'slighted', which in this case was done by gutting the interior. The north wall had been breached by Roundhead cannon; and, as the ruin thereafter stood entirely neglected, the damaged wall, or the greater part of it, finally collapsed on Christmas Day 1910. Sixteen years later the remains were made over to the custody of the then Office of Works, by whom the stone work was repaired, the wide moat re-excavated and filled anew with water. Unfortunately, in the interval most of the fallen masonry, which otherwise might have been re-set, had become the prey of local greed.

The tower-house forms a rectangle on plan, with stout drum towers at all four corners, so managed that they reduce the two gable walls of the main building to a mere strip. It contained four storeys, all the floors being wooden. In the middle of the north wall is the entrance, above which is seen a slot through which passed the chain for lifting the drawbridge. The ground floor contained the kitchen, with a draw-well. On the first floor was the common hall, and above it the lord's hall, and finally the solar. A straight mural stair ascends from the entrance passage to the lower hall; and at the north-east angle of the latter a spiral stair mounts to the lord's hall. How the solar was reached is not now apparent—probably by a stair in the vanished north wall. All the rooms are well appointed, in a rich Gothic style. The wide easy stair in the north-east tower is a late insertion. In the south-west tower the uppermost chamber was the chapel. Its super-altar, with the usual five consecration crosses, remains in the breast of the east window, and beside it a canopied niche contains the piscina. Externally, the tower-house forms an architectural composition of fastidious beauty. It is built of the finest polished ashlar. The wall-heads are crowned by a boldly oversailing machicolated parapet. Within this, on the four towers, rises an inner cylinder; and these cylinders, as we learn from a sketch made by a Cavalier officer in 1644, were crowned with tall conical helmets, while the main structure had a high-pitched roof with dormer windows. All this is thoroughly French in manner: the inner cylinder of the four drums we have already met with in the great towers at Warwick Castle (p. 25). Remains of a large outer enclosure to the north and west of the moated tower-house doubtless represent the *domus Elye de la Mare apud Nuny*, on record in 1264. With its venerable parish church, its imposing and beautiful castle, and the snug village that grew up round these twin *foci* of paternal feudalism, the ancient manor of Nunney, lovely in itself, enjoys a lovely setting.

The design of Nunney Castle has led to some discussion. The late Sir Charles Peers wrote as follows:

> In spite of its small scale it is still rather a castle than a fortified house, and is really to be considered as an example of the rectangular courtyard plan, with a round tower at each corner, such as may be seen in the contemporary work at Farleigh Hungerford. At Nunney, owing to the nature of the site, the plan has been telescoped, as it were, and its corner towers are set close together in pairs at either end of an oblong building of four storeys, which contains the whole living accommodation.

This opinion of Peers is entitled to the utmost respect. In the case of another tower-house of about the same age as Nunney, that of Warkworth (pp. 34-5), I have shown that its design is in fact that of a courtyard castle of the Bodiam type, in which the courtyard has become atrophied, as it were, into a central lantern. But at Warkworth the living accommodation is arranged horizontally round this central void —kitchen, hall, great chamber and chapel following each other in the normal medieval sequence, just as at Bodiam. By contrast, Nunney is strictly a tower-house, in which the rooms are piled on top of each other, and there is no central lantern. It hardly seems possible, therefore, to think of Nunney Castle as a 'telescoped courtyard'. While the crowning of the four drums undoubtedly shows French influence, it does not seem necessary to seek, as some have done, a model abroad for the plan; since, as we have seen (p. 32), in the early fourteenth century Sir John de Somery had built himself a tower-house of the same outline on top of his *motte* at Dudley.

9
Castles in Brick

When the town of Hull, one of the *villes neuves* founded by Edward I, was fortified anew towards the end of the fourteenth century, its walls, with their thirteen towers, were built of brick. A tower or curtain wall made of this material is not necessarily weaker than one built of stone. Most of the castles erected by the Teutonic Order in the lands which they conquered eastward from the Vistula were constructed out of this material; and they include some of the strongest and most formidable medieval fortifications to be found anywhere in Europe. The largest and grandest of them all, the Grand Master's castle at Marienburg, withstood a seven weeks' bombardment during the Second World War. Though terribly battered, it nevertheless survived, and is now in process of restoration. In England, probably our earliest brick building[1] is Little Wenham Hall, a semifortified manor house in Suffolk, built in the closing years of Henry III. By the fifteenth century the new material was in common use, and has enriched our castellated architecture with a group of splendid buildings, of which it must suffice in this book to give some account of only six: Caister, Herstmonceux, Tattershall, Buckden, Oxburgh and Kirby Muxloe. In all of them, though foreign brickmasons from the Low Countries and the Rhineland were sometimes used, the bricks themselves were locally produced.

CAISTER CASTLE in Norfolk stands on low ground about four miles northward from Great Yarmouth. Interest has always attached to the

---

[1] We are not here thinking of such a castle as Colchester where Roman bricks have been largely re-used in the masonry.

castle owing to the facts that it was built by the famous Sir John Fastolf—the original of Shakespeare's Falstaff, though the hard-bitten warrior of history was a very different character from the scallywag of the dramatist's humour; and that it played a part in the chequered fortunes of the Paston family, so brilliantly illuminated by their vast correspondence. The ruins, with their tall slender tower, have also attracted attention as an early and splendid example of brickwork; and added interest is furnished by the partial survival of the building accounts, covering the period 1432–5.[1] Unfortunately these accounts tell us nothing about the architect. This is the more regrettable as the plan of the castle is unique in this country, and clearly is based upon a Rhenish *Wasserburg*, such as Schloss Kempen in the lower Rhineland, to which it bears a compelling resemblance. We must therefore regard it as a product of the close connexion, during the fourteenth and fifteenth centuries, between England, the Rhine Palatinate and the Hanseatic League, with which the Rhenish towns were affiliated.

The central and principal part of the castle consists of a rectangular building, lying roughly east and west, and enclosing a courtyard. At the north-west angle of this building is an immensely tall, slender round tower, boldly projected; and in the middle of either front, east and west, are gatehouses. Of these, the western is covered by a walled forecourt, containing on its south side a long edifice, at the south-west corner of which is a low round bastion tower. On the east side is a second large forecourt, also walled, with round towers at the two outer angles, and ranges of buildings along three sides, east, north and south. The central building and the eastern forecourt were enclosed by a wide ditch, with a cross-cut separating these two portions. From the western forecourt a wide low arch admitted to the 'barge ditch', an artificial channel which emptied itself into the River Bure. 'By this channel', to quote a writer of 1760, 'goods, etc were more easily conveyed to and from Yarmouth than by land', the road formerly betwixt Caister and Yarmouth being 'very bad, and in winter almost impassable'. Of all this great fabric sadly little now remains. The eastern forecourt survives only in fragments of its walls; the building in the western forecourt has been adapted to form a comfortable modern country house: while of the central building the principal survival is the astonishing angle tower,

[1] For Caister Castle see *Antiquaries' Journal*, vol. XXXII, pp. 35–51; and, for the building accounts, *Norfolk Archaeology*, vol. XXX, pp. 178–88.

perhaps the most dramatic thing of its kind in England. No more than 23 feet in diameter, it rises to a height of almost 100 feet, reckoning to the summit of its hexagonal stair turret. The tower proper is crowned by a machicolated parapet of brick arches and corbels, in groups of three divided by a panel of brickwork corbelled out at a lower level. By simple means this device produces a rich effect. Beneath the parapet is a row of circular gunloops. Similar provision for the new defence by hand-guns is found elsewhere in the castle. Much refinement is shown in the stonework dressings, which are entirely English in character. One brick fireplace shows a moulding found commonly in Baltic brickwork. The brick-workings still exist on the river a mile and a half below the castle. They cover an area of no less than four acres.

So early as the reign of Edward I there was a moated manor-house at Caister. Here Sir John Fastolf was born about 1378. On 18 June 1381, this early dwelling was seized, looted and damaged during the Peasants' Revolt. The eastern forecourt of the castle is built of a different kind of brick, with a considerable admixture of flint rubble: its walls are thinner, and the loop-holes are of a kind not found elsewhere in the castle. It is not impossible that this walling may be a relic of the older manor-house. In his new castle Sir John Fastolf died in 1459, bequeath-ing his lands in Norfolk to Sir John Paston. But ten years later Caister, in the absence of the new owner, was besieged and captured, with the aid of cannon, by the Duke of Norfolk. After the castle had been 'sore broken with guns of the other party', the scanty garrison honourably surrendered. Eventually Sir John Paston recovered his inheritance, and the family continued to enjoy Caister until 1659. But the castle does not seem to have played any further part in history, and indeed ceased to be occupied in the last year of the sixteenth century.

HERSTMONCEUX CASTLE in Sussex, now the official residence of the Astronomer-Royal, has long been justly celebrated as one of the most beautiful of English baronial buildings; as an early example of the use of brick upon a vast scale; and as a magnificent parade of brow-beating feudal pride, erected at a time when the paraphernalia of defensive architecture, while still to some extent functionally purposed, were employed rather as an outward and visible symbol of seigneury—a demonstration of arrogance on the part of a ruling class whose martial

traditions required that they should house themselves in mansions where the semblance of armed defiance was preserved, even in a countryside in which a serious attack was perhaps no longer to be feared.

Here, also, as at Caister, an older manor-house stood upon the site. Early in the thirteenth century it belonged to a family who took their name, de Herst, from the place, but soon adopted the additional surname of de Monceux, apparently from a barony near Bayeux, with which they were presumably connected. Both Henry III and Edward I visited this older manor-house. Before 1331 the property passed to Sir John de Fiennes, whose fourth successor, Sir Roger Fiennes, like Sir John Fastolf, a veteran of the French wars, obtained in 1441 a licence to 'enclose, crenellate and furnish with towers his manor of Herst Monceux'. His descendants continued to hold the manor until 1708, becoming in succession Lords Dacre of the South and Earls of Sussex. In the early eighteenth century the castle was occupied by the celebrated Bishop Francis Hare. After his death in 1740 it was neglected. In 1774 the interior was gutted, and its materials used to build on to a neighbouring house, now known as Herstmonceux Place. In 1911 a new owner, Sir Claude Lowther, began to restore the castle, and the work was completed by his successor, Sir Paul Latham. The new interior buildings follow lines entirely different from the original dispositions. In the present brief sketch we shall therefore concern ourselves chiefly with the external cincture of walls and towers. Concurrently with the restoration, the wide enclosing moat was partly filled anew with water.

At all four corners of the immense quadrangular pile are boldly salient octagonal towers; from each of the north, west and east fronts three semioctagonal towers project; while on the south or entrance front, which measures 208 feet over all, the semi-octagonal towers again number four, but the central pair are set close together as a gatehouse. This gatehouse is one of the most imposing pieces of quasi-military architecture in Britain. The portal is set beneath a deep and lofty arched recess, which contains the two long slots into which the gaffs of the drawbridge worked back. Beneath the arch a row of 'murder-holes' covers the entrance. Above, the angular towers are developed by corbels into cylinders; and both towers, with the wall between them, are crowned with a boldly oversailing machicolated parapet of brick arches carried forward on great stone corbels. Behind

31 Herstmonceux Castle, entrance from the moat

this parapet, there rises from each tower an inner cylinder, such as we have already noted at Warwick and Nunney. The total height of this majestic gatehouse is about 84 feet. Provision for defence with both firearms and archery is made by means of gunloops and bowslits.

The middle tower on the north front contains a postern gate, likewise set in a deep recess and covered overhead by a machicolated parapet. Here also the moat was spanned by a drawbridge, with slots to receive the gaffs.

While the castle as a whole is built of brick, the mouldings and dressed work are for the most part executed in stone—greensand, apparently from Eastbourne.

As to the original interior arrangements, known from excellent plans and drawings, I have elsewhere pointed out the close connexion which obviously exists with Eton College, and have suggested that William Veysey, 'brickmaker and King's sergeant', who was in charge of the work at Eton College in 1442–3, was also responsible for the building of Herstmonceux. As Treasurer of the Household to Henry VI, Sir Roger Fiennes would have much to do with providing the financial wherewithal for Eton, and can hardly have failed to come into contact with Veysey.[1] Normally in a large mansion of the later Middle Ages the buildings are grouped around two courts, the living apartments compactly disposed around an upper court, while the offices and out buildings, more loosely articulated, were relegated to a basecourt. We have already studied this disposition at Farleigh Hungerford (p. 102). By contrast, Sir Roger Fiennes, through his ingenious design of internal courts and connecting galleries, consolidated all his household requirements into one vast embattled framework. Was this in obedience to defensive requirements? To some extent, perhaps, yes. But it also meant an enormous gain in practical convenience, and in the strict oversight of a numerous household. The late Mr Holland Walker gave the name of 'laager plan' to the type of castle illustrated at Herstmonceux. No term could be more happily chosen: for the root idea is that of a fortified quasimilitary household. From such documents in the fifth Earl of Northumberland's Household Book we know how minutely organised, how strictly disciplined and time-tabled, was the domestic establishment of a great nobleman of the later Middle Ages.

[1] See my paper on Herstmonceux Castle in *Archaeological Journal*, vol. XCIX, pp. 110–22.

The advantages, in supervision, maintenance of order, and avoidance of waste, obtainable by encompassing such a household within a single fenced rectangular framework, in principle like a Roman fort, are too obvious to require labouring. It was those same advantages that governed the plan of an Oxford or Cambridge college: and therefore it is no coincidence that collegiate ideas of planning have so plainly influenced the original interior dispositions of Herstmonceux Castle.

A century later than Herstmonceux, another large brick castle on the 'laager plan' was built at Kirby Muxloe in Leicestershire. This will come more properly for discussion in the next chapter. Meantime we turn to consider the most astonishing piece of fifteenth-century brick-work in England—the great tower added to his castle of TATTERSHALL in Lincolnshire, between 1434 and 1446, by Ralph, first Lord Cromwell, Lord High Treasurer of England. He was a man of vast wealth and a magnificent builder, as appears not only by his works at Tattershall, but also by the stately residence which he erected for himself at his other property of Wingfield in Derbyshire. At Tattershall Lord Crom-well carried out a complete reorganisation of the manorial centre. His operations may be summarised as follows. He added a second moat round his thirteenth-century castle, providing a pleasance with fish ponds. The early domestic buildings were in part reconstructed and in part replaced; and, as thus reorganised, they comprised a great hall with a two-storeyed annexe containing a parlour and upper chamber; kitchens and offices; and a chapel. To the west side of these buildings, and connected with them by corridors of access on the ground and first floors, Lord Cromwell added, as his own private residence, the colossal tower-house which alone of all these stately structures now survives, and is the glory of Tattershall—beyond any doubt, as Lord Curzon has said, 'the most splendid piece of brickwork in England'. In the two outer wards were various buildings, including a wool-house and a large stable. Cromwell's household at Tattershall was on a lavish scale, for we are told that it consisted of at least a hundred persons. Lord Cromwell also pulled down the old parish church and replaced it, after the manner of his age (which we have already seen at Warkworth, p. 37), by a collegiate establishment. His new church was not com-pleted till the end of the century. Fortunately, though now bereft of the stained glass which once made its interior a glory of colour, the great cruciform church still survives as perhaps the finest of all the Lincolnshire churches that remain as a memento of the wool-based prosperity of the eastern counties in the fifteenth century.

The mighty tower-house which Lord Cromwell added to the old castle of the de Tateshales is one of the most astonishing architectural achievements that the Middle Ages have bequeathed to us in any country. The walls are built of red brick made from the local Kimmeridge clay, but the dressed work is all of green or red Salmondby sandstone or limestone from Ancaster. At all four corners of the lofty tower are stout octagonal turrets, which rise above the main building and finish with crenellated parapets carried forward on brick corbels and pointed archlets. The main building, which is four storeys high, above a basement below the courtyard level, has a heavy oversailing machicolated parapet resting on enormous stone corbels united by trefoliated archlets also of stone. Above this the wallheads are organised in two stages. The lower, opening in a series of arches from the flat roof, has a row of square-headed and traceried windows to the field, and forms a covered way from which the *mâchicoulis* were served. The upper stage, or wall-walk proper, has a crenellated parapet. The west face of the tower, overlooking the moat, with its splendid suite of Perpendicular traceried windows, has been designed as the 'show front'. The eastern face, towards the courtyard, was of course masked in its lower portion by the two tiers of corridor connecting it with the adjoining building. The joist-holes and roof-plate of this corridor annexe still remain.

Internally the tower-house contains a dark store in the basement. On the first floor is a large and stately hall, having no communication with the upper floors, and clearly meant as a court of justice, like the corresponding room of the great tower-house in the archiepiscopal palace at Sens. Here Lord Cromwell, or in his absence his bailiff, would preside over the feudal courts of the barony of Tattershall. Above this are successively the lord's hall, *camera*, and solar. The two lower of these are reached by long corridors in the thickness of the east wall. The interiors of the tower are all appointed in the most sumptuous manner, with many minute and interesting details illustrating the constructive ingenuity and artistic skill devoted to its building. Space forbids me to do more than merely to mention the three magnificent heraldic fireplaces, the finest of their kind in England. The story of how these mantlepieces were torn out for export to America, how Lord Curzon intervened, bought Tattershall, retrieved the fireplaces, restored the castle, and bequeathed it to the nation, when reckoned along with his similar work at Bodiam, may serve to remind us of the social usefulness of a class whom we have high authority to praise: 'rich men furnished with ability, living peaceably in their habitations'.

The disappearance of all the other buildings to which it was once attached has left this great tower standing stark and lonely. Its present isolated position, and the unusual splendour of its design, have always aroused wonder. Many have been the speculations about its real purpose, and the source from which Lord Cromwell derived the idea of so remarkable a structure. Most of these speculations have been coloured by fanciful analogies between the fifteenth-century brick tower-house and the rectangular stone keeps of Norman and Angevin times. Under this misconception, it has been usual to think of Lord Cromwell's tower house as a kind of conscious architectural atavism, 'an imitative reversion to the Norman style'. On the contrary, it is in the forefront of contemporary fashion in the secular architecture of western Europe. It is exactly paralleled in such a building as the donjon of the *Palais de Justice* at Poitiers, built by the Duc de Berry between 1382 and 1388. Here we find a lofty rectangular tower, in this case of stone, with a round tower at each corner, the whole edifice being crowned with a machicolated parapet. Here, as at Tattershall, the tower-house formed the lord's residence, and is in contact with a large hall which served the general purposes of his household. Here, as at Tattershall, the disengaged face of the tower is developed as a 'show front'. An even closer parallel is to be seen in the Grand Master's palace at the castle of Marienburg, added to the older building between 1380 and 1390. Here we have the same association of a lofty tower-house, containing private accommodation, with an earlier hall. The two are linked together with a corridor of access, similar to that at Tattershall. Externally the palace, with its ponderous buttresses recalling the turrets at Tattershall, its strongly developed 'show front' and its great oversailing machicolated coronet, has unmistakable affinities with the Lincolnshire tower. Both are built of brick, and there are striking resemblances between them in the minor details of mouldings, diaper work, groined vaulting, and the general management of the brickwork. The palace at Marienburg was built by the great architect Klaus Fellenstein, who came from Koblenz. Now the Tattershall building accounts, which have most fortunately been in part preserved[1], reveal that the master brick-mason was *Bawdwin Docheman*, usually translated as Baldwin the Dutchman. But in the fifteenth century, and for long thereafter, the word Dutchman meant often not Dutch but Deutsch. It may signify anybody of Teutonic origin; so Baldwin may have come from anywhere within the German area. In Lord Cromwell's time the Hanseatic merchants in London were regularly known as Dutchmen; and it would be easy to compile a long list of instances, including brickmasons, from the fifteenth and sixteenth centuries, of the word Dutch in the sense of German. It may not be without significance that Koblenz, which sent Klaus Fellenstein to build his masterpiece at Marienburg, was an important commercial and cultural link between England and Germany.

The building accounts tell us much of interest about the sources of the various materials. The bricks were made at Lord Cromwell's kilns, partly at Boston but mostly at Edlington Moor, a few miles north of Tattershall. Here the pits from which the clay was dug may still be seen, as well as a fragment of the 'Tower on the Moor', evidently built to supervise and protect the workmen. Production was on an enormous scale: well over a million bricks are accounted for in the pay rolls, so far as these have been preserved.

Inevitably so dramatic an edifice as Tattershall, being also the first of its kind in England, found its imitators; and it has long been recognised that the small group of brick towers in the eastern Midlands are copies on a reduced scale of the Tattershall theme. In particular the intimate connexion between Lord Cromwell's great tower and the very similar structure which was added, about a generation later, by the Bishops of Lincoln to their palace at BUCKDEN, in Huntingdonshire,[2] has often been remarked. What is specially interesting is the fidelity with which the episcopal builders at Buckden had copied, not merely Lord Cromwell's tower, but the whole lay-out that he devised with such splendid *élan* at his Lincolnshire seat. Taken together, the two *ensembles* form

---

[1] Published by the *Lincoln Record Society*, vol. 55.
[2] See *Journal Brit. Archaeol. Ass.*, 3rd ser., vol. II, pp. 121–32.

a remarkable picture of late medieval ideas in the reorganisation of a capital messuage. In each the domestic buildings, instead of being ranged along the curtain wall as was the ancient practice, are projected into the

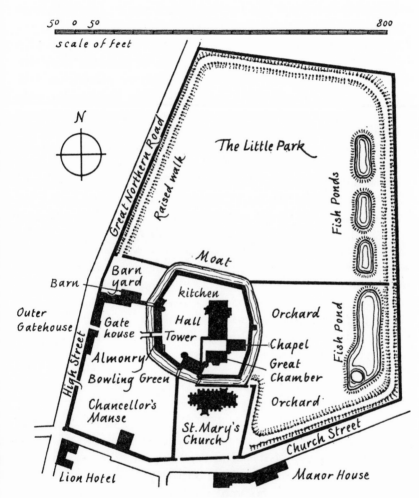

Plan of Buckden Palace

courtyard. In each is attached to these domestic buildings a great brick tower, oblong in plan with octagonal turrets at the corners. In each this tower is set on the line of the curtain, so that its outer wall is washed by the moat. Both castles also have a large outer enclosure, containing a pleasance and fishponds. Lastly, at both places the manor is intimately associated with a splendid church. At Tattershall, as we have seen, Lord Cromwell replaced the old parish church by a collegiate establishment. At Buckden the church was not demolished, and its parochial status never altered. But it was extensively rebuilt, so that, in its main features, it is now a fifteenth-century edifice.

Very obviously, both at once to the eye and upon a study of its plan and details, the Buckden tower, though smaller and simpler, has been inspired by that at Tattershall. There is the same oblong plan, with octagonal corner turrets, the same bold plinth, the same marking out of the storeys by string courses, the same flat roof and open embattled parapets, alike on tower and turrets. The 'show front' is not emphasised to the same degree as at Tattershall, but the grouping of the windows on either side of a large and monumental chimney breast, and the handsome trifoliated decorative niche sunk in the latter at first floor level, provide a somewhat similar effect. The Buckden tower has only four storeys, but presents an advance upon its prototype in having a second newel stair. There are no parallels at Buckden to the mural chambers and corridors which are so remarkable a feature at Tattershall. Nor was any attempt made to reproduce the browbeating machicolated coronet which is the glory of Lord Cromwell's tower. At Tattershall the wall-head arrangements have still a serious defensive value. How completely any such idea was absent from the mind of the Buckden master-mason is shown by the fact that his wall-heads are overlooked, at a distance of no more than 50 feet, by the much higher parapet of the church tower.

We are told by John Leland that it was Bishop Rotherham (1472–80) who 'builded the new brick tower at Buckden. He clene translatid the haul, and did much coste there beside'. The function of such a tower as the lord's private residence is clearly brought out by the fact that in the Parliamentary survey of Buckden, drawn up in 1647, the tower is styled the 'King's Lodging'. Henry VIII stayed more than once at Buckden, and no doubt occupied the tower, which will thus have obtained this name. We are reminded of Pitscottie's account of Holyrood: King James V, he tells, 'foundit ane fair palice in the Abbay of Hallieroodhous and ane great towre to himself to rest into quhene he pleissit to come to the town'. Such a great tower, in the later Middle Ages, was not architectural antiquarianism, no harking back to Norman ideas: it was a natural and proper form for the residence of a magnate,

32   Tattershall Castle from the east

combining the three basic requirements of outward magnificence, ample accommodation, and privacy.

Henry VIII's ill-used wife, Katharine of Aragon, was sent to Buckden after the infamous 'divorce' in 1533; and in her 'great chamber' there, in December of that year, took place the dramatic interview with the Duke of Suffolk, when he attempted to persuade her to adopt the title of Princess Dowager, and she (to quote the Duke's report to his royal master) 'before all the servants of the house protested with open voice that she was Henry's Queen and would rather be hewn in pieces than depart from the assertion'. The servants, who stiffly stood in their conscience 'that Katharine was Henry's Queen,' and no man sworn to serve her as Queen might change that oath 'without perjury', were 'committed to the porter's ward, there to remain without speaking to anyone, till the King's pleasure was known'.

Lastly let us look for a few minutes at OXBURGH HALL, on the margin of the Norfolk Fens, the ancient seat of the Bedingfield family. Here, pursuant to a licence granted in 1482, Sir Edmund Bedingfield built himself a large quadrangular mansion of brick, enclosing a courtyard and girt by an ample moat. A generous array of windows, some of them handsome oriels, look out on all sides across the water. Despite the fact that many of these openings are modern, or at least have been altered in modern times, it is obvious that, apart from the considerable obstacle imposed by the moat, the only serious defence is offered by the stately gatehouse. This rises to a height of no less than seven storeys in its pentagonal flanking turrets, with between them two full storeys above the arched portal. At base the towers have crosslet loopholes with spade-shaped lower terminals. They are crowned with open crenellated parapets, while high over the entrance there is a long *mâchicoulis*. Inside the courtyard, which is reached through a rib-vaulted passage, the rear arch of the portal is flanked by pentagonal battlemented turrets. But these are not carried up as far as the parapet of the main structure, which has three ornamental stepped gables and is flanked by embattled octagonal turrets, also showing crosslets with spade-shaped terminals. While all this martial apparel is not entirely innocent, it is clear that the designer's aim has been to give the outward show and imposing effect of castellar construction, rather than the stern reality of older days. Plainly in this building we see the English castle on its way out—still clinging to something of its menace, and dignified to the last.

33 Kirby Muxloe Castle, south west tower

Internally, the dispositions are quite traditional, with the great hall on the side opposite from the gatehouse. Originally this must have been a noble stateroom, with an oaken hammer-beam roof which an eighteenth-century writer likens to that of Westminster Hall, 'and being lately very agreably altered and improved may be justly accounted one of the best old Gothick halls in England'. Unfortunately in 1778 the entire southern range of the quadrangle—kitchen, hall, great chamber, and dining parlour—was taken down by Sir Richard Bedingfield. Thereafter the quadrangle stood open until the missing range was inadequately replaced in the nineteenth century. Sir Richard also rearranged the other apartments round the courtyard. Fortunately he spared the gatehouse. On the first floor of this there is a large and well-appointed hall, quite in the manner of some of the medieval gatehouses with which this book will have made the reader familiar. It is now known as the King's Hall; yet no English sovereign is certainly known to have visited Oxburgh. Access to this gatehouse hall, and to the upper floors of the gatehouse, is obtained by a fine brick spiral stair in the north-west tower. A notable feature of this stair is the stone sunk handrail, an ingenious device which had already been used at Tattershall. Such stone-moulded handrails, let into the staircase wall or the newel, are common in France in the fifteenth and sixteenth centuries. The finest one I have seen is in Francis I's open staircase at Blois.

The ancient castle of the Bedingfields has had much to endure. It underwent its final bout of 'restoration' in the early nineteenth century, when the demolished south range was replaced, but only to a height of one storey, though the south-east corner was carried up tower-wise in quite an effective fashion. Honourable mention is likewise due to the brick garden wall, with its array of embattled square towers. Oxburgh Hall contains many treasures, notably the famous needlework hangings bearing the monogram, coat of arms and other insignia of Mary Queen of Scots, and almost certainly, in part at least, her own handiwork.

The scenic exaggeration of the gatehouse, so evident at Oxburgh Hall, was reproduced early in the next century with even greater flamboyance at Layer Marney Hall in Essex, where the gatehouse towers are carried up to a height of no less than eight storeys. Here, however, we have left the Middle Ages behind us; for although the mansion is built in general of traditional English red brickwork, Italian craftsmen were called in to make the windows, parapets and other decorative features out of cream-hued terracotta, and in the style of the Italian Renaissance. But our chronicle of the English castle is not yet complete. So in our final chapter we must turn back to consider a group of formidable strongholds deriving their origin from the turbulence and revival of militarism that culminated in the Wars of the Roses.

IO

Bastard Feudalism and the Latest Castles

Every student of English history in the fifteenth century is aware of the serious political and social evil caused here, as in France, by the armed retainers of the powerful lords; how the widespread and chronic anarchy erupted finally into the Wars of the Roses; and how energetically thereafter the Tudor monarchs beat it down in their stringent statutes against 'livery' and 'maintenance'.[1] The mischief had already become acute in the latter part of the fourteenth century: the first Act against 'livery' was passed in 1377, the first against 'maintenance' so far back as 1327. In the overseas wars the English barons had only too aptly learned their lesson from their French antagonists. Instead of vassals they now surrounded themselves with armed retainers, each clad in his lord's livery and bound to fight for him in his private quarrels: while the lord on his part pledged himself to 'maintain' them against all legal consequences of their misdoing, either by suborning or bullying juries, or, when that failed, by yet more violent means. Matters drifted from bad to worse after the English were turned out of France, and large numbers of unemployed ex-service men, habituated to lawlessness, were only too glad to accept the livery of a powerful lord. Bishop Stubbs has summed up the matter in his usual luminous manner:[2]

> The old feudal spirit which prompted a man to treat his tenants and villeins as part of his stock, and which aspired to lead in war, to judge and

---

[1] See above, pp. 61-2, for Henry VII's stern treatment of his host at Hedingham.
[2] *Constitutional History of England*, vol. III, pp. 530-1.

to tax, his vassals without reference to their bond of allegiance to the Crown, had been crushed before the reign of Edward III; but the passions to which it appealed were not extinguished, and the pursuits of chivalry continued to supply some of the incentives to vanity and ambition which the feudal customs had furnished of old. The baron could not reign as king in his castle, but he could make his castle as strong and as splendid as he chose; he could not demand the military services of his vassals for private war, but he could, if he chose to pay for it, support a vast household of men armed and liveried as servants, a retinue of pomp and splendour, but ready for any opportunity of disturbance; he could bring them to the assizes to impress the judges, or to parliament to overawe the king; or he could lay his hands, through them, on disputed lands and farms, and frighten away those who had a better claim. He could constitute himself the champion of all who would accept his championship, maintain their causes in the courts, enable them to resist a hostile judgment, and delay a hazardous issue. On the seemingly trifling pomp and pretence of chivalry, the mischievous fabric of extinct feudalism was threatening gradually to reconstruct itself.

To this illegitimate offspring of the old age of the feudal system the name of 'bastard feudalism' has been given. Such retainers—'bastard feudatories'—lived inside their lord's castle, or at least within its purlieus. They had their meals at his board, their liveries from his wardrobe, their swords, spears, knapsculls and jacks from his armouries, their horses out of his stables. It was with mercenary armies thus raised that the Wars of the Roses were fought out—the bloodiest and most unprincipled internecine conflict in our whole long history. Let us now see what effect this latest, aberrant development of feudalism exerted on a group of formidable castles erected during this stormy time.

William, first Lord Hastings, was one of the principal actors on the Yorkist side in the tangled drama of the Wars of the Roses. At home and abroad he held numerous exalted posts, including those of High Chamberlain of the Royal Household, Receiver of the Duchy of Cornwall, Master of the Mint, Chamberlain of North Wales, Lieutenant of Calais, and Ambassador, on various occasions, to Scotland, France, Brittany and Burgundy. From his vast estates, the emoluments and exploitation of his offices, and substantial pensions which he did not scruple to accept from the King of France and the Duke of Burgundy, he enjoyed enormous wealth, and was one of the foremost builders of his time. Like all the nobles of this turbulent period, he kept his private army. Thus in 1474 we find him entering into a bond with two lords, nine knights, and forty-eight esquires, who pledge themselves to aid him against all persons within the kingdom, and to raise as many men as they can, to be armed at his expense. It is no matter for surprise that such a man, in the sumptuous scheme which he adopted for the re-contruction of his castle at ASHBY-DE-LA-ZOUCH in Leicestershire, should provide for himself a self-contained tower-house on a great scale—not out of any antiquarian hankering to imitate a twelfth-century keep, but simply to have in his castle a strong isolated residence where he could keep himself, his family and his personal household apart from the crowd of armed retainers whose services he bought with his ample purse, and upon whom he rested the formidable power that he brought to bear amid the shifting politics of his time.

The licence to crenellate in respect of Ashby was issued to Lord Hastings on 17 April 1474. The manor-house which he inherited there dated mostly from the twelfth and fourteenth centuries. It comprised the normal lay-out of a large central hall, on the basilican plan, with nave and side aisles, having buttery, pantry, and kitchen at its lower end, and at its upper end the solar, beyond which was a fine chapel. All these buildings were extensively reconstructed by Lord Hastings, who drew them together into the northern side of a large courtyard en-closure, screened by a massive curtain wall. Midway in the south front of this he placed the mighty tower-house that is the glory of Ashby-de-la-Zouch, and the structure with which we are at present chiefly concerned.

Beautifully built of the finest sandstone ashlar, the tower measures 48 feet by 41 feet, over walls 8 feet 6 inches thick, and when it stood entire rose to a height of fully 90 feet. From the middle of its east front projects a square wing, carried up to the full height of the main building. The latter contains four storeys, and in the wing there are seven, the lowest only being vaulted. In the basement of the main building is a vaulted store, on the first floor is the kitchen, likewise vaulted, while above are successively the hall and great chamber. Opening off the hall is a beautiful little oratory in the north-west turret. The entrance, defended by a portcullis, is at ground level in the north wall. In the north-east corner a spiral stair serves all the floors both in the main tower and in the wing, terminating on the wall-walk. Beneath the stair-foot is a small vaulted 'pit' or prison. The architectural appointments of the building are of the most magnificent description, the groined vaulting of the kitchen being as fine as anything of its kind and scale in England. Externally the tower forms a composition of unusual richness and dramatic force. The wall-head finishes with a bold machicolated parapet, and at each angle are tall octagonal corbelled turrets, carried through two full storeys, and elaborately ornamented. The machicolations are united by archlets, a mannerism derived from France.

Here, then, we have a structure not differing in function, though varying in form, from the tower-houses which we have already studied at Dudley, Nunney and Warkworth. And as in their case, there is nothing atavistic about it. We may be sure that Lord Hastings, a practical and up-to-date man of affairs, would have been entirely unenthusiastic had his master-mason proposed to build him 'a tribute to the memory of the ancient keeps'. On the other hand, it is equally wide of the mark to compare it with the tower at Tattershall. We have seen that Lord Cromwell's tower there does not form a complete, self-contained seigneurial residence standing by itself, but is simply a glorified solar block, attached to a pre-existing house, and at ground level quite unsecured. Moreover, its martial garniture is largely for appearance's sake. It is mere *appareil féodal*, put there to portray the pomp and pride of the lord. In marked contrast to all this, the great tower at Ashby forms a self-contained and isolated residence for the owner. While it has plenty of the pride and pomp of feudalism, it is yet strictly and formidably a military proposition, a true product of its times and and of its builder's special needs. It was with no idle use of language that the parliamentary commissioners of 1648 reported on 'the Great Tower of Ashby-de-la-Zouch, being a place of considerable strength'. They knew what they were talking about: because its capacity for resistance, against an artillery such as Lord Hastings had never feared, had recently tasted the stress of siege. The respect which the Great Tower had earned from its assailants is shown by the fact that after its capture they partly blew it up.

At the beginning of this book I wrote about Sir Walter Scott's *Ivanhoe*, and the profound influence which that famous romance has exercised in fixing the popular ideas about the Middle Ages. It is hardly necessary to remind my readers that Ashby-de-la-Zouch is the scene of the 'gentle and joyous passage of arms'. Indeed the very site of the fictitious tournament is marked on the map with the Gothic lettering that the Ordnance Survey reserves for antiquities! In introducing his readers to the castle, Sir Walter declares that

> this was not the same building of which the stately ruins still interest the traveller, and which was erected at a later period by the Lord Hastings, High Chamberlain of England, one of the first victims of the tyranny of Richard III, and yet better known as one of Shakespeare's characters than by his historical fame.

Nevertheless, as I have mentioned above, quite a lot of the present fabric dates back to the early Plantagenet period; and in particular the noble hall may be accepted as the place where Prince John is supposed to have given the famous tournament feast, in the course of which the Prince and his Norman favourites behaved so rudely to his Saxon guests.

Save for the fact that his lot was cast in more unquiet times, which brought him to a bloody end, the career of Lord Hastings in not a few respects resembles that of his predecessor, Ralph, Lord Cromwell. Just as Cromwell built or rebuilt stately houses for himself at his three chief manors of Tattershall, Wingfield and Collyweston, so we find Lord Hastings carrying out a similar programme at Ashby-de-la-Zouch, Kirby Muxloe, and Bagworth. This similarity of programme extends also to the materials used—and even, as it chances, to the present position of both these groups of great houses. Of Bagworth and Collyweston, next to nothing now remains: but Ashby-de-la-Zouch and Kirby Muxloe answer, in the second half of the fifteenth century, to Wingfield and Tattershall in its earlier half. Each pair in its period represents impressively the most advanced ideas of late medieval castellar construction. And just as Cromwell built at Tattershall in brick and at Wingfield in stone, so Hastings varied his material at Ashby and at Kirby Muxloe. Only in the case of Wingfield does the building magnate appear to have started with a *tabula rasa*. At all three other places an older house occupied the site, and the way in which in each case it was dealt with forms not the least interesting point in any study of the group. Our immediate concern is with the contrast between Lord Hastings' two castles, Ashby and KIRBY MUXLOE, also in Leicestershire.

34   *Ashby-de-la-Zouch Castle*

At Ashby, as we have seen, Hastings built in fine ashlar from the local Carboniferous sandstone—an excellent building material which Cromwell had already used to some extent, at Tattershall. At Kirby Muxloe, on the other hand, Hastings chose brick. To supervise his undertaking here, he brought over from Tattershall, where Hastings was one of the curators of Lord Cromwell's will, the master-mason John Couper, who was in charge of the building of the collegiate church then in full progress there. The records now available about John Couper enable us to salute him as one of the foremost English architects of the later Middle Ages. He continued to reside at Tattershall, where the great church demanded his constant presence: but he came over frequently to supervise the work at Kirby. It is most fortunate that the building accounts of Kirby Muxloe have been preserved in their entirety, and enable us to follow every detail of the work, week by week, from the commencement on Monday 23 October 1480, when the first forty cartloads of fuel were delivered at the brick kiln, until Monday 6 December 1484. The news of Lord Hastings' death, on 13 June 1483, reached Kirby three days afterwards; and subsequently work had proceeded on a much reduced scale. In the end the castle was left uncompleted, probably very much as we see it today. But during all those four years every penny of expenditure, whether in wages of men or in purchase of materials, is faithfully recorded. If the good clerk's Latin failed him, he woud help himself out with French or English. So we have one delicious entry: *una mucfforke empta pro le fferming*. Here, in six words, we have all three main ingredients which have mixed to make the English language.

At Kirby Muxloe, as at Ashby-de-la-Zouch, an older house occupied the site when Lord Hastings began his operations. As at Ashby, this house comprised the normal disposition of a central hall, with buttery, pantry and kitchen at its lower end, and at the upper end a large solar— off which, at right angles, extended a range of living rooms. From the building accounts we learn that this house was set within a towered curtain wall, and that the whole establishment included an inner and an outer court, in the old-fashioned manner that we have studied at Farleigh Hungerford. But whereas at Ashby these early buildings were preserved and remodelled by Lord Hastings, at Kirby, save for one wing, they were removed *pari passu* with the growth of the new edifice. So the early curtain and towers disappeared; but the foundations

35 Raglan Castle

of the domestic buildings still remain within the later courtyard, and have been laid bare by excavation. At Ashby, Lord Hastings was content to refashion the domestic buildings, while adding a novel element in the mighty tower-house which, as we have seen, was his response to the strain placed upon his establishment by the abnormal social conditions of the time. At Kirby, on the other hand, the fortified mansion which John Couper designed for his noble patron is a perfect example of the contemporary 'laager plan'. Here also for the first time in England, as it would seem, systematic provision was made for defence by hand-guns—though, to be sure, the provision made is, from a practical standpoint, sometimes naive enough.

Kirby Muxloe Castle, then, consists of a large quadrangular building enclosing a courtyard, and girt about by a wide, deep moat. At all four corners were square towers, lofty and bold. A square tower also projected from the middle of three sides of the castle, while on the west side was the gatehouse. Angle towers and gatehouse were of three storeys; intermediate buildings seemingly of only two. The hall and kitchen appear to have been in the eastern range. Unfortunately of this once extensive structure nothing now remains above the foundations, with the exception of the gatehouse, which survives to a height of two storeys, and the south-west tower, which is complete. The gatehouse is a rectangular structure with pentagonal towers flanking the portal, and similar but smaller towers on the courtyard face. The entrance was approached across the moat by a bridge, and was defended by drawbridge, portcullis, and folding doors. The inner portal was defended by a second pair of folding doors, closing against the courtyard quite in the Edwardian tradition. The first floor contains a single large apartment, but two fireplaces and the disposition of the windows declare that this was subdivided. From the building accounts we learn that the gatehouse was to have been crowned by a machicolated parapet.

A remarkable feature about this castle is the patterned brickwork. Diapering of 'burnt ends' had been tentatively employed at Caister, Tattershall, and elsewhere: but here this kind of ornamentation—*pictura* it is termed in the building accounts—is most elaborate, including the initials W.H., for William, Lord Hastings, and the *maunch* or hanging sleeve which is the heraldic bearing of the family. It is noteworthy that this decorative work was entrusted to foreign brickmasons, whose names suggest that they were sometimes of Flemish or Germanic stock.

The tragic end of Lord Hastings is familiar to everyone through Shakespeare's *Richard III*. Without even the pretence of a trial, and upon the most frivolous pretext, he was arrested during a Privy Council in the Tower, hurried downstrairs into the courtyard, and there and then his head was hacked off upon a log:

> O bloody Richard! miserable England!
> I prophesy the fearfull'st time to thee
> That ever wretched age has looked upon.
> Come, lead me to the block; bear him my head;
> They smile at me who shortly shall be dead.

Plantagenet blood flows in the veins of the ducal house of Beaufort; for it descends from Henry Beaufort, who was a great-grandson of John of Gaunt by his mistress, Catherine Swineford. This Henry Beaufort, third Duke of Somerset, had a natural son, Sir Charles Somerset, who in right of his wife, Elizabeth, heiress of the Herberts of Raglan in Monmouthshire, was summoned to Parliament as Lord Herbert. In 1514 he was created Earl of Worcester. It was Henry Somerset, first Marquess of Worcester, who,—true to his own proud motto, *mutare vel timere sperno*—gained himself undying glory by his defence of RAGLAN CASTLE in the cause of Charles I. A man of vast wealth, he maintained a household staff of 150, and had two belted knights as his stewards. Out of his own resources he is said to have provided the King with nearly a million of money (value of the time!) towards the cost of the struggle against the House of Commons. In addition to this, he bore the whole charges, £40,000, of the stubborn defence of his castle, which he maintained with the utmost skill, gallantry and resolution against every effort of the Roundheads, until at last their heavy cannon, which included mortars firing twelve-inch shells, breached the walls, and the stout old Cavalier, on 19 August 1646, surrendered with all the honours of war. Parliament commemorated the fall of the castle by declaring a public holiday. The Marquess was then close on seventy years of age, and his health had been shattered by the rigours of the siege. From prison he addressed a petition to the House of Commons, praying that, since his life could not in any case be prolonged for many days, he might be granted the last boon of dying free. The docket attached to this pathetic request may be left to speak for itself: 'Read, 16 Dec., 1646; nothing done; dead, 18 Dec., 1646'. Parliament made some amends by giving him a stately funeral—the cost of which, £500, they charged against his estate. And, within a fortnight of its capture, word had gone forth to 'slight' the old Royalist's ancestral home. Its splendid fittings were torn out and sold, the strong old walls were overthrown, and ever since it has remained a broken and a silent ruin— one of the most magnificent and loveliest of English castles. In 1938 the Duke of Beaufort placed the ruins under the guardianship of the Commissioners of H.M. Works, and the castle is now maintained as a national monument.

In its ruined state Raglan Castle exhibits a remarkable commixture of military and domestic architecture. The thick and lofty outer walls with their proud array of multangular towers, crowned with over-sailing machicolated parapets, and the massive detached hexagonal keep or citadel—the so-called 'Yellow Tower of Gwent'—which is girt by its own moat, wide and deep and lined with stone: these portions date from the fifteenth century, and preserve the martial garniture of that warlike time. But alongside all this brow-beating militarism we find the richly decorated domestic buildings of the Tudor and Stuart period—the great hall, dining room, gallery and chapel, dividing the interior of the castle into two large courts, of which the outer or Pitched Stone Court contained the kitchen and offices, while the inner or Fountain Court was surrounded by the state apartments, served by a noble perron or outside staircase. Behind this, reached through a postern gate, was a long bowling green and a terrace decorated with statues of the Caesars. A remarkable thing about the castle is the superb ashlar masonry out of which both the earlier and the later portions are mostly built. The ruins, now embosomed in fine old timber, remnants of the ancient demesne, stand midway in the open rolling champaign country that separates the valleys of the Usk and Wye.

With its double courtyard, upper and lower, Raglan Castle plainly does not belong to our 'laager' type. In not a few respects, indeed, it was built upon an outmoded design. Particularly is this true about the 'Yellow Tower of Gwent'. Here, if anywhere, we may truly speak of a 'reversion to the ancient keeps'. Part of the explanation must doubtless be sought in the fact that the huge hexagonal tower is built, like the

Kenilworth keep, round the core of a Norman *motte*, of which it is probable that the rest of the castle may represent the original bailey. Yet it is well equipped with gun-ports, as well as crosslet loopholes for archery. The tower, which is unvaulted, contained the traditional accommodation: a kitchen, with a well in the basement; the lord's hall on the first floor; solar above; and bedrooms doubtless over all. A single spiral stair, rising from basement to wall-head, served the whole structure. This astonishing edifice is known to have been built by Sir William ap Thomas about 1432–45; while the wide-spreading cincture of curtain walls and towers was the work, between 1450 and 1460, of his son William Herbert, Earl of Pembroke, a prominent supporter of the Yorkist cause. Here also a notable feature is the ample provision of gunports.

This magnificent castle has long fired the imagination of its beholders. Towards the end of the fifteenth century a Welsh poet, with Celtic exuberance, extols its 'hundred rooms filled with festive fare, its hundred towers, parlours and doors, its hundred heaped-up fires of long-dried fuel, its hundred chimneys for men of high degree'. And in 1587 an English visitor describes it thus:

A famous castle fine
That Raggland hight, stands moated almost round:
Made of freestone, upright as straight as line,
Whose workmanship in beauty doth abound.
The curious knots, wrought all with edged tool
The stately tower, that looks over pond and pool;
The fountain trim that runs both day and night
Doth yield in show a rare and noble sight.

As I have already said, the Tudor monarchs struck hard and repeated blows against the evil of 'bastard feudalism'. 'As to riot and retainers', wrote Bacon in his *Historie of the Raigne of Henry the Seventh*, 'there passed scarcely any parliament in his time without a law against them'. The Court of Star Chamber was specially erected by King Henry to deal with the menace of private armies; and the last act of Parliament against 'maintenance' and 'livery' was placed on the statute book in 1504. Yet the practice was deep ingrained and hard to kill. One of the latest exponents was Edward Stafford, third Duke of Buckingham. Men said that he 'would be a royal ruler'. He had appointed officers on his lands (so it was alleged in his indictment), for the purpose of retaining men, and had accumulated arms and habiliments of war, with a view of fortifying himself against the King. It is not surprising that his castle of THORNBURY in Gloucestershire, left unfinished by him at his execution in 1512, should be perhaps the last major baronial house in England designed as a serious fortification. The main building was laid out upon the traditional plan of a four-square edifice enclosing a court-yard and having an outer court of retainers' lodgings and offices. This retainers' court is a most astonishing structure. It forms a veritable barracks, containing stabling on the ground floor and well-appointed living rooms overhead, reached by outside wooden stairs. From the exterior, its long sweep of walls and towers, well provided with cross-lets and gunloops, gives something of the impression of a town *enceinte*. From the open country it is entered by a regular gatehouse with frontal and rearward towers, the portal between which was still, even at this late date, provided with a portcullis.

The western or entrance front of the main castle contains the gate-house, likewise furnished with a portcullis. This imposing 'fore-face', with its central gatehouse between two massive towers, and its ponder-ous angle-towers, of which the only one completed is tall and crowned by a business-like machicolated parapet, has much of the character of a fourteenth-century castle, and not a little of its stern reality. Crosslet loopholes and gunports complete the sense of menace. It is clear that Duke Edward's castle, while providing an imposing effect of which its builder was doubtless fully conscious, was also meant to be, like William of Deloraine—that bold retainer—'good at need'. Yet on the southern front, where stood the Duke's residential quarters, we find that all semblance of defensive architecture has vanished. Large and beautiful oriel windows open on the ground floor; and doubtless the master-builder and his noble patron found it easier to discard considerations of security on this side, because here the castle is covered by a massive embattled outer wall enclosing the privy garden, beyond which lie the parish church and graveyard. But since Thornbury was left in-complete by the Duke's attainder, we do not know what his final plan for the castle may have been.

Nevertheless, enough of the main building survives to enable us, with the aid of two surveys, one made by the royal commissioners after the forfeiture, and the second in 1562, to understand fairly clearly the ideas that underlay the Duke's arrangements. We do not find here

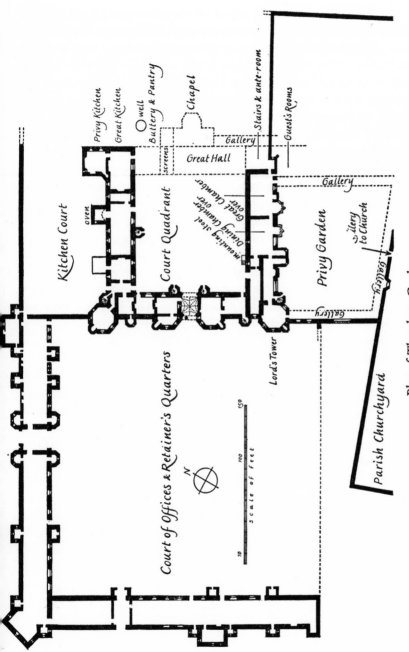

Plan of Thornbury Castle

the traditional uninterrupted deployment of kitchen and offices, great hall and solar apartments, running clockwise round the court. For his south range violates this sequence. It starts from the opposite end. Instead of following on from the great hall, the lord's suite is set back to back with it. Let us remember that at Bodiam the two suites, the retainers' and the lord's, similarly turn their backs upon each other. At Thornbury, as at Bodiam, the lord's suite forms an independent, self-contained quarter. The great south-western tower was clearly designed as a private and secure post, in case of need a refuge, for the owner its thick internal walls must have made it almost fireproof. In case of necessity, the posterns at its base and on the first floor would afford the owner means of escape.

With Thornbury, therefore, we reach the final manifestation of the fortified houses of the overmighty subject, designed to accommodate his private array of armed retainers. The incomplete state of the castle today may serve as a symbol of the abrupt, drastic way in which the Tudor monarchy called halt to the evil practices summarised in contemporary terms, 'livery' and 'maintenance'. This becomes the more certain when we compare Thornbury Castle with Cowdray House, built some ten or twenty years later. At Cowdray the gatehouse and frontal angle towers have only the external appearance or make-belief of such. They do not form separate or tower-like units in the internal plan: indeed, on the upper floors, the gatehouse is open to the range extending north from it. Thus the castellated aspect of the main front is a sham; and this despite the antique phraseology of the licence granted in 1533 to its owner, to 'embattle and fortify, crenellate or machicolate, those walls and towers'. Here, as not infrequently before and since, the crown lawyers have failed in their language to keep abreast of the times.

36   Carew Castle, south side

11

The Fighting Finish of the English Castle

I believe it may be true to say that Thornbury was the last English castle to be built with a serious purpose of defence. For the future, the wealthy landowners of Tudor and Jacobean times were content to built themselves stately country houses, in which only the moat was sometimes retained, perhaps more as a symbol of consequence, even of amenity, than for any security it could offer in the settled government of Queen Elizabeth. Where a landowner had inherited a medieval castle, he might either desert it for a new, uncastellated residence; or he might seek to modernise it in accordance with current ideas. The latter course produced some ingenious and charming results. We have already noted one such case at Dudley. Let us now look at another example, CAREW CASTLE, in Pembrokeshire.[1]

Early in the twelfth century the lordship of Carew was held by Gerald of Windsor, constable of Pembroke Castle. Since the latter is only five miles distant, it is doubtful whether Gerald had a castle or manor-house of any consequence at Carew. But recent investigation has identified the remains of a small square gate-tower, attributable to the twelfth century, in the middle of the east front of the present castle. This tower, like the corresponding, much larger, early gatehouse at Ludlow, was later converted into a keep by walling up both ends of the entrance passage. Towards the close of the thirteenth century what was virtually a new castle, upon a much larger scale, was erected by Sir

[1] The name is accented on the first syllable.

Nicholas de Carew, a notable soldier whose mailed effigy remains in the parish church. Despite much later transformation, the work of Sir Nicholas remains the core of the castle as now we find it. It consists of an irregular 'quadrant court', entered by a simple gatehouse on the 'forefront' towards the east, and defended at the four corners by powerful round towers. Of these the western pair are particularly grand, rising from great basal spurs in the form of half pyramids meeting below, so that the actual ground-plan of the tower is a square. This is a common south Welsh mannerism: for example, it forms a conspicuous feature in the group of towers on the northern sector of the great barrage at Caerphilly. Along the west side of Sir Nicholas de Carew's courtyard was the common or retainers' hall: opposite to it, on the entrance front, was placed the lord's hall, his private rooms above and a handsome chapel in a protecting pentagonal tower, which covers the entrance from its right flank—where the assailants were unprotected by their shields. This frontal position of the lord's suite, and the close control of the gatehouse thereby provided, is of course entirely in accordance with Edwardian ideas.

In the reign of Henry VII Carew Castle was remodelled by Sir Rhys ap Thomas, one of the original, and to the end unswerving, supporters of the first Tudor monarch. It is beyond our purpose to consider in detail his work at Carew. Suffice it to mention here the superb presentation, over the principal entrance from the courtyard to the western range, of the armorial bearings of his royal patron; the King's son, Arthur Prince of Wales; and the latter's wife, Katherine of Aragon, for whom her husband's untimely death reserved the tragic destiny of becoming the first Queen of Henry VIII. It was at Carew Castle, this newly re-fashioned, that Sir Rhys ap Thomas in 1507 held his famous tournament, the grandest ever mounted in Wales. Sad to say, Sir Rhys ap Thomas' grandson incurred the jealousy of Henry VIII, and in 1531 perished on the block. In 1558 his forfeited estates were granted to Sir John Perrot by Queen Elizabeth, whom he had conspiratorially supported against her half-sister, Queen Mary. Later Sir John became Lord Deputy of Ireland. Nevertheless towards the end of his benefactor's reign he was condemned to death for treason, but died in the Tower before the Queen had decided upon his fate. His son was allowed to succeed, but upon his death the Queen bestowed Carew upon her favourite, the Earl of Essex.

Sir John Perrot's principal alteration upon Carew Castle was the replacement of the older north range by the magnificent Elizabethan suite which, with its double tier of mullioned and transomed windows, its great two-storeyed semicircular oriels, and its eastern bow, forms such a notable feature of the ruins as seen across the tidal creek of Milford Haven upon which Carew Castle is placed. One thing that will strike the visitor is the absence in Perrot's building of any visible sanitary provision. This is quite common in Elizabethan houses. It does not imply a decline in domestic standards. Commodes were now used, and were much more hygienic than the mural privies and shafts of the Middle Ages, with their lack of means of flushing.

Obviously Perrot's work must have greatly reduced the military strength of the castle. Nevertheless, during the Civil War it put up a prolonged and stout resistance to the Roundheads, until in September 1645, it yielded to their cannon. A stone ravelin thrown up by the defenders upon the eastern front remains a silent witness to the siege, of which little is otherwise known. Thereafter the castle was put out of action by blowing up the south curtain. But the living quarters, though damaged in the siege, continued to be inhabited, though upon a much reduced scale, until the Revolution of 1688.

Every visitor to Carew Castle has to pass the noble wayside cross which survives as perhaps the finest monument of that Celtic Christian civilisation of Wales which contrasts so favourably with that of her early Anglo-Norman invaders. Its tall tapering shaft, reduced by two offsets before it is crowned by a graceful open wheel-cross, is richly decorated with panels of fretwork and interlaced patterns; and the monument, which is over 13 feet in height, bears an inscription recording that it commemorates Maredudd ap Edwin, King of Deheubarth (South Wales), who was slain in 1035.

Carew is only one among many examples, some already mentioned in this book, which show that our medieval castles, even if sometimes weakened by Tudor and Jacobean improvements, could still offer an obstinate resistance to the cannon of the new era. Their stout old walls, furbished up and often protected by external bastions or ravelins, proved themselves capable of holding out tenaciously against the siege tactics of the time. Most of them were held for the King against the

Parliament: and we have seen how at Scarborough, Ashby, Raglan and other places, they went down fighting and suffered the inevitable end of demolition at the hands of the conqueror. In another book[1] I have described at some length the treatment thus meted out to Corfe Castle in Dorset after its long and heroic resistance. The sheer bad temper thus provoked among the victorious Roundheads led to the use of mine and gunpowder to an extent far exceeding what was necessary to render the castle in a military sense untenable.

So today Corfe Castle remains as perhaps the most vivid and dreadful picture in England of the devastation caused by the Civil War.

Unfortunately the records of siege operations in that ruinous strife are tantalisingly incomplete. For example, at Caerphilly, though we saw that a Civil War redoubt still remains, and that the castle has plainly been destroyed with gunpowder, no record of the siege seems to have come down to us. So also Pickering Castle in Yorkshire has likewise been obviously dismantled; but of its fate nothing is known, save for the statement of an eighteenth-century topographer that 'when it was besieged by the Parliament's forces, a large breach was made on the west side of it; and after it was taken, great quantities of papers and parchments, several of which had gilt letters on them, were scattered about the street called Castle-gate, and were picked up by the children who were attracted by the glittering leaves'. By contrast, other sieges, such as that of Raglan Castle, or the epic two-years' defence of Basing House, which its gallant owner, the Marquess of Winchester, re-christened 'Loyalty', are well-known. Let us therefore conclude this book by considering briefly a less celebrated yet notable Civil War siege, the records of which are unusually full.

DONNINGTON CASTLE, near Newbury in Berkshire, was built by the lord of the manor, Sir Richard Abberbury, pursuant to a licence to crenellate granted by Richard II in 1385. The site which he selected for his castle—if indeed there had not been a pre-existing manor-house there —was the summit of a hill overlooking the River Lambourne, about a mile north of Newbury. Conformably to the ideas of its time, the castle consisted of a roughly quadrangular enclosure, but bulging outward into a salient upon the western front. At the four main angles were round towers, small but boldly projected; and midway in the east front

---

[1] *Exploring Castles*, pp. 137–42.

a tall gatehouse with two round towers. Of the rest of the building little but the foundations now remain, but fortunately the gatehouse survives almost complete. It forms a rectangular block, from which the two round towers project strongly, both forwards and upwards. These towers show a graceful 'batter', or inward taper, emphasised by five projecting string courses, of which the third and fourth are embellished by grotesque heads. The towers are embattled, and so is the gatehouse, the first floor of which contains the portcullis chamber, lit by a handsome window, over the head of which the third stringcourse on the towers is brought up and across. The storey above contains a living room, lighted by a larger and traceried window, similarly framed by an upward stepping of the stringcourse. Both towers have simple vertical loopholes, but no windows. In the south tower is a spiral stair. The portal is a depressed pointed arch, well moulded. Within, the entrance passage is groin-vaulted. The gatehouse behind now forms part of a modern dwelling. In front of the gatehouse there has been a small forework, enclosing a drawbridge pit. The material of the gatehouse is coursed flint and chalk rubble. Altogether this is one of the most graceful and stylish buildings of its time and kind. Embosomed in fine old elm trees, it makes upon the visitor an impression as charming as it is unexpected.

In 1415 Sir Richard Abberbury sold Donnington to Thomas Chaucer, son of the poet, and for a time Speaker of the House of Commons. Later it passed through his heiress Alice, successively into the hands of her three husbands: Sir John Phellip; Thomas Montagu, a distinguished soldier, who was killed by a cannon ball at the siege of Orléans in 1428; and William de la Pole, Duke of Suffolk, who, after being defeated before Orléans by Jeanne the Maid, had the good sense to make peace with France in 1444, but paid for his statecraft by an outburst of public indignation which led to his seizure at sea, while crossing over to France. His captors threw him across the gunwale of their boat and hacked off his head with six strokes of a rusty sword (2 May 1450). Head and body were thrown out upon the beach at Dover. In retrospect, this barbarous deed can be seen as the curtain-raiser of the Wars of the Roses. Alice Chaucer and her ducal husband left a son—a lad of eight, who was brought up at Donnington and inheriting (as it would seem) the deft matrimonial policy of his mother, became the husband of Elizabeth Plantagenet, sister of Edward IV. On the downfall of the de la Poles in the reign of Henry VII, Donnington was forfeited to the Crown. It is unnecessary here further to trace the devolution of the manor. But, apart from the glory which it obtained in the Civil War, Donnington Castle is remarkable through the illustrious magnates who have been its lords.

At the outbreak of the struggle between King and Parliament, Donnington belonged to a Puritan M.P., John Packer. His castle was seized by the Royalists, who considered it an important post, covering Oxford from the south, and commanding the main road to Bath.

In the first battle of Newbury (20 September 1643) Donnington Castle played no part. But after the battle the castle was fortified and garrisoned by order of the king, the command being entrusted to Colonel John Boys, later to be knighted for his heroic defence. As the ancient building was of course unable to withstand cannon, Sir John, in the course of the two and a half years during which he held his command in face of the enemy, constructed an outer defence of gabioned and timbered earthwork, with angle bastions. The remains of these are yet visible, as also are the siege works constructed by the Roundheads, including north, south, and south-eastern batteries, and a redoubt and stockaded musketry pit towards the south east. At the commencement of the siege, the garrison was estimated at about 200 infantry, 25 horse, with no more than four guns. Against Donnington the Roundheads brought up heavy ordnance, and in a twelve-days' bombardment destroyed the southern curtain along with its three flanking towers. In a vigorous sortie the garrison invaded the siege works, destroyed the gabions, and brought back a large amount of arms and ammunition. It was partly to relieve Donnington that King Charles came down from Oxford and fought the second battle of Newbury (26 and 27 October 1644) which took place almost under its walls, and in which the castle guns afforded material assistance to the royal army. After the battle King Charles left his artillery, ammunition and baggage, with a number of his wounded, inside the defences of Donnington. But the Roundheads soon gathered again before the castle. A summons to surrender was accompanied by the threat that if the offer was not accepted, the besiegers would not leave one stone of the castle upon another. 'If so', tersely replied Sir John Boys, 'I am not bound to repair it'. With a large force the King once more relieved the castle, and retrieved the guns and baggage which he had left there after the recent battle, including the State Crown, the Great Seal of England, much treasure, and his private correspondence. At the same time the defences of

Donnington were strengthened, so that the artillery now amounted to a couple of dozen pieces, including five or six heavy guns. By this time it had now become a matter of prestige for the Roundheads to reduce the castle, though they could easily have invested it closely and awaited the effect of starvation. The task of assaulting the castle was offered to Cromwell, who respectfully declined undertaking 'such a knotty piece of business'. A sum of no less than £6600 was voted by Parliament towards the expenses, and a considerable force was assembled, along with a formidable siege train, including a fifteen-inch mortar. A last gallant sortie failed to dislodge the attackers. The great mortars smashed what remained of the castle to bits; the defenders' guns were dismantled, and their earthworks rendered untenable. And so the Governor, having been allowed to send out a messenger to obtain his royal master's permission, on 30 March 1646, laid down his arms in honourable surrender. His resources had been reduced to six serviceable pieces of ordnance, twenty barrels of powder, and 140 men, It is on record that the motto *Loiaulte oublige* was freely displayed in the stained glass windows of the castle; and surely the injunction had been faithfully obeyed by Sir John Boys and his heroic few. Today the worn earthworks and shattered remnant of Donnington Castle remain, to quote the inscription on his tomb, as 'a noble monument of his fame'.

Upon this high note the present book may aptly close. The castles of England had had their day. Some few have been kept up for national purposes. Quite a number still survive as habitable mansions, in some happy cases still occupied by the descendants of their builders. But mostly they are deserted, silent ruins, haunted by the memory of many of the proudest and some of the most shameful episodes in our long and chequered national history:

> And there they stand, as stands a lofty mind,
> Worn, but unstooping to the baser crowd,
> All tenantless save to the crannying wind,
> Or holding dark communion with the cloud.
> There was a day when they were young and proud;
> Banners on high, and battles passed below;
> And they who fought are in a bloody shroud,
> And those which waved are shredless dust ere now,
> And the bleak battlements shall bear no future blow.

Index

The numbers in *italics* refer to illustrations

Abberbury, Sir Richard   166, 167
Allington Castle   8
Appleby Castle   80, 81, 82
Arthur, Prince   84, 164
Ashby-de-la-Zouch   1, 7, 152, 153, 154, 155, 156, 166, *34*
Astor of Hever, Viscount   9, 10
Avignon   127
Aydon Castle   132, 133

Baldwin the Dutchman   144
Bamburgh Castle   67, 68, 69, 70, *14*
Barbour   75
Barnwell Castle   91, 92, 93, 94, *18*
Barons' War   67
Bastide   82, 92, 107
Bayeux Tapestry   4, 28
Beaufort, Duke of   158
Beaumaris Castle   116, 117, 118, 120
Bedingfield, Sir Edmund   147
Bedingfield, Sir Richard   148
Belsay Castle   127, 128, 129, 130, 131

Bodiam Castle   95, 96, 97, 100, 101, 133, 134, 135, 143, 162, *20*
Boleyn, Anne   9, 10
Boleyn, Sir Thomas   10
Bolton Castle   98, 100, 101, 133, *22*
Boys, Sir John   168, 169
Brakspear, Sir Harold   32
Brough Castle   *23*, 82
Brougham Castle   23, 82
Buckden Palace   136, 144, 146
Buisli, Roger de   43
Bute, Marquess of   8
Bute, Lord   124

Caernarvon Castle   109, 111, 112, 113, 114, 115, 116, 119, 120, 121, 122, 123, 124, 125, *25*
Caerphilly Castle   119, 122, 123, 164, 166, *28*
Caister Castle   136, 137, 138, 139, 139, 156, *30*
Caldicot Castle   15, 17, 18, 25, 29, 78, *4*
Cardiff   47
Carew Castle   163, 164, 165, *36*

Carew, Nicholas de 164
Castle Rising 70
Cerceau, Jacques Androuet du 7
Charles I 57, 115, 134, 157, 168
Château Gaillard 87, 105, 126
Chaucer, Alice 167
Civil War 20, 40, 75, 111, 115,
  124, 165, 166, 168
Clare, Gilbert de 120, 123
Clark, George T. 83
Claudius, Emperor 55
Claverings 34
Clifford, Lady Anne 23, 82
Clifford, Roger de 38, 82
Clifford's Tower 39, 7
Clinton, Geoffrey de 18
Colchester Castle 53, 54, 55, 56,
  57, 58, 61, 62, 65, 15
Conisbrough Castle 2, 16, 71, 72,
  73, 74, 88, 111, 119, 12
Constantine the Great 112, 113
Constantinople 115
Conway Castle 111, 119, 24
Corfe Castle 13, 23, 42, 69, 166
Coucy, Château de 107
Couper, John 155, 156
Cromwell 75, 76, 77, 169
Cromwell, Lord 141, 142, 143,
  144, 155
Curzon, Lord 97, 141, 143

Dallingrigge, Sir Edward 95
Daubeny (de Albini), William 67
David II, King 69
Denbigh Castle 119, 120
Donnington Castle 166, 167, 168,
  169, 37
Dover 13, 14, 70
Dudley Castle 31, 33, 34, 35, 135,
  153, 163
Dunstanburgh Castle 124, 125

East Prussia 92
Eden, River 9, 81
Edward I 1, 13, 15, 53, 74, 91, 92,
  104, 107, 110, 111, 113, 118, 119,
  120, 128, 138, 139
Edward II 17, 24, 32, 38, 43, 47,
  65, 75, 115, 116, 122, 123
Edward III 17, 43, 69, 74, 95, 115,
  133, 151
Edward IV 47, 70, 84
Edward VI 91
Eleanor of Aquitaine 43
Eleanor of Castile 43
Elizabeth I 1, 20, 101, 118, 163,
  164
Ethelfleda 45
Eton College 140

Farleigh Hungerford Castle 101,
  103, 134, 135, 140, 155, 21
Fastolf, Sir John 9, 137, 138, 139
Fellenstein, Klaus 144
Fiennes, Sir John de 139
Fiennes, Sir Roger 9, 139, 140
Fitz-Turstin 51
Flint Castle 105, 106, 107, 108,
  111
Framlingham Castle 89, 90, 91, 19

Gaveston, Piers (Earl of Cornwall)
  65
Gerald de Barry 87, 88, 89, 92
Gerald of Windsor 163
Gloucester, Duke of 17, 29
Gloucester, T.R.H. the Duke and
  Duchess of 94
Glyndwr, Owain 115
Gotch, J. A. 7, 127
Green, John Richard 92, 129
Greville, Sir Fulk 25, 26

Harlech Castle 116, 117, 118, 122, 124, *27*
Hastings 52, 95, 109
Hastings, Lord 151, 152, 153, 155, 156, 157
Hatton, Sir Christopher 23
Haughton Castle 126, 127
Hautkoenigsbourg 8
Hawkesworth, Colonel 22, 23
Hedingham Castle 58, 59, 60, 61, 62, 64, 66, *9*
Henry I 90
Henry II 8, 43, 48, 53, 64, 90
Henry III 18, 40, 43, 66, 69, 105, 127, 128, 139
Henry IV 38, 108
Henry V 24, 102
Henry VI 30
Henry VII 61, 75, 77, 159, 164, 168
Henry VIII 5, 9, 17, 23, 84, 118, 146, 164
Henry of Ellerton, Master 111
Herstmonceux Castle 8, 136, 138, 139, 140, 141, *31*
Hever Castle 8, 9, 10, 26, *3*
Hitcham, Sir Robert 91
Holy Sepulchre, Church of the 85
Honnecourt, Villard de 93
Hope, Sir William St John 84
Hull 92, 136
Hundred Years' War 32, 53, 133
Hungerford, Sir Thomas 101, 102, 103
Hungerford, Sir Walter 102

Isabella—'She-wolf of France' 17, 123
Ivanhoe 1, 2, 3, 7, 153

James I 25, 35

James of St George 104, 105, 109, 111, 115, 116, 118, 119
John, King 18, 67, 69, 76, 91
John of Gaunt 17, 18, 22, 23, 43, 95, 101

Katharine of Aragon 147, 164
Kempen, Schloss 137
Kenilworth Castle 15, 18, 20, 21, 22, 23, 24, 159, *5*
Kenilworth, Lord 20
Kirby Muxloe Castle 136, 154, 155, 156, *33*
Krak des Chevaliers, Le 105

Lancaster, Earl of 74
Latham, Sir Paul 139
Latimer, Bishop 91
Launceston Castle 78
Layer Marney Hall 148
Leicester, Robert Earl of 20, 22, 23
Leland, John 98, 146
Lewes Castle 40, 41, 42, *8*
Lewyn, John 98
Lisle, Sir George 57
Little Wenham Hall 136
Llanbeblig 113
Llanstephan Castle 124, 125
Lloyd, Nathaniel 7
Longtown 78
Lucas, Sir Charles 57
Ludlow Castle 82, 83, 84, 86, 163, *16*

Macsen Wledig 113
Magna Carta 91
Magnus Maximus 112, 113
Manorbier Castle 87, 88, 92
Mare, Sir John de la 133
Marienburg 136, 143

Marlowe 24, 65
Marshal, Earl 15, 16
Marshal, William 76, 77
Marshall, Thomas 132
Mary, Queen of Scots 101, 148
Mary Tudor 91
Maurice the Engineer 70
Meschines, Ranulf de 81
Middletons of Belsay 128
Monck, Sir Charles 130
Montfort, Simon de 18, 25, 40, 42, 51, 67

Newbury, Battle of 168
Newcastle-upon-Tyne 70
Norwich 70
Nunney Castle 133, 134, 135, 140, 153, 29

Offa, King, 44, 45
Oman, Sir Charles 122
Oxburgh Hall 136, 147, 148
Orford Castle 71, 72, 73, 74, 13
Oxford, Earl of 61

Parnell, James 57
Paston, Sir John 138
Peasants' Revolt 67, 138
Peers, Sir Charles 135
Pembroke Castle 74, 75, 17
Pembroke, Earl of 75, 76, 77
Penchester, Sir Stephen 9
Perrot, Sir John 164, 165
Pickering Castle 166
Pierrefords 8, 25
Pleshey Castle 29, 31, 37
Porchester Castle 22
Publicius 113

Radford, Dr Ralegh 49

Raglan Castle 21, 157, 158, 166, 35
Rees, Professor William 121
Restormel Castle 48, 49, 50, 51, 58
Rhuddlan Castle 109, 110, 111, 23
Richard I (Coeur-de-Lion) 1, 4, 105, 126
Richard II 17, 95, 98, 108, 109, 111
Richard III 18
Richard, Earl of Cornwall 51
Richmond, Countess of 75
Ridley, Bishop Nicholas 91
Rochester Castle 65, 66, 71, 11

Scarborough Castle 62, 63, 64, 65, 95, 166, 10
Scott, Sir Walter 1, 3, 13, 27, 45, 74
Scrope, Richard Lord 98
Segontium, 112, 113
Shakespeare 23, 38, 53, 157
Sharington, Sir William 33
Shirburn 133
Shute, John 33
Somery, Sir John de 31, 32, 135
Stafford, Edward, Duke of Buckingham 5, 17, 159
Stephen, King 8, 11, 48, 69, 84
Stubbs, Bishop 150
Suffolk, William de la Pole, Duke of 167
Surrey, Earl of 82

Tacitus 55
Tattershall Castle 136, 141, 142, 143, 144, 146, 153, 154, 155, 156, 32
Tamworth Castle 44, 45, 46
Taylor, Arnold 117, 118

Teutonic Order   136
Theodosius, Count   63
Thomas, Sir William   159
Thomas, Sir Rhys ap   164
Thornbury Castle   5, 160, 161,
   162, 163
Thorpe, John   5, 7
Tickhill Castle   42, 43
Tipping, Avray   7
Tonbridge Castle   124, 125
Tout, Professor   80
Tower of London   13, 53, 91, 105,
   119
Toy, Sidney   48, 50
Tretower Castle   78, 79
Tudor Act of Union   109

Valence, Aymer de   75
Veysey, William   140
Ville neuve   82, 92
Viollet-le-Duc   25

Wales, Statute of   109

Walker, Holland   140
Walter of Hereford   111
Warrenne, William de   40
Warrenne, Earl   67, 74
Wars of the Roses   12, 25, 61, 69,
   149, 150, 151, 167
Warwick Castle   15, 18, 24, 25,
   26, 140, *6*
Warkworth Castle   34, 35, 36, 37,
   38, 82, 135, 141, 153, *1*
Westminster Abbey   39
William the Conqueror   24, 38,
   52, 65, 69
William II   69, 75
Willoughby, Sir Francis   5
Windsor, St George's Chapel   37,
   47
Wingfield   141, 154
Wollaton Hall   5, 6, *2*
Wyatville, Sir Jeffry   7

Yanwath Hall   131, 132, *26*
York Castle   38, 40, 41